General editor: Graham Ha

Brodie's Notes on

W. B. Yeats:
Selected Poetry

W. T. Currie BA and Graham Handley MA PhD

MACMILLAN

First published 1978 by Pan Books Ltd

This revised edition published 1992 by
THE MACMILLAN PRESS LTD
Houndmills, Basingstoke, Hampshire RG21 2XS
and London
Companies and representatives
throughout the world

ISBN 0-333-58223-3

Typeset by Footnote Graphics, Warminster, Wiltshire
Printed in Great Britain by
Clays Ltd, St Ives plc, Bungay, Suffolk

Contents

To the student   4

Preface by the general editor   5

The author and his work   6

Critical introduction   9
1 Yeats and symbolism   9
2 Ireland: the country and its politics   10
3 Maud Gonne   12
4 Magic and the occult   13

**Poem summaries and commentaries and
textual notes**   16
from **Crossways** (1889)   16
from **The Rose** (1893)   20
from **The Wind among the Reeds** (1899)   29
from **In the Seven Woods** (1904)   34
from **The Green Helmet and other poems** (1910)   37
from **Responsibilities** (1914)   40
from **The Wild Swans at Coole** (1919)   46
from **Michael Robartes and the Dancer** (1921)   54
from **The Tower** (1928)   59
from **The Winding Stair and other poems** (1933)   70
from **Words for Music Perhaps**   76
from **A Woman Young and Old**   79
from **A Full Moon in March** (1935)   81
from **Last Poems** (1936–1939)   83

**Revision questions (including note-form
guideline answer)**   92

Further reading   94

These Notes are based on the Pan edition of
W. B. Yeats: Selected Poetry, but references are
made to each individual poem, so the Notes may
be used with any edition of the book

To the student

This book of notes is an introduction to the poetry of Yeats. There follows a chronology of his life, together with an indication of some of the guidelines to be used in reading his poetry. But Yeats was essentially an esoteric, idiosyncratic poet who was at times obscure: do not be deterred by apparent obscurity; for sometimes the form, the manner of writing, the language, the imagery, may have a private meaning for the poet or the person learned in his lore, yet convey another meaning or aspect of experience to another, uninitiated reader. This is the joy of Yeats, for even when he is obscure he is compelling. Tease out meanings, associations, responses as you read; find out what you can about him from books like T.R. Henn's *The Lonely Tower* and from Yeats's own prose writings. In a book of this length the authors cannot define the meaning of every word, nor would they wish to do so. Half the joy of poetry comes in discovery, whether imaginative or literal, and the other half comes in the experience or emotional response, which may not even be possible to rationalize. Read to enjoy, to experience, to share, to discover – and you will find Yeats a perfect guide. He speaks to us across the years – and, remarkably, more clearly and passionately as an old man than when he was young. Accept the challenge, for Yeats is the master of the unusual, the paradoxical, the mystical, the unknown: his great virtue is that he invites the reader to share in all these.

Preface by the general editor

The intention throughout this study aid is to stimulate and guide, to encourage your involvement in the book, and to develop informed responses and a sure understanding of the main details.

Brodie's Notes provide a clear outline of the play or novel's plot, followed by act, scene, or chapter summaries and/or commentaries. These are designed to emphasize the most important literary and factual details. Poems, stories or non-fiction texts combine brief summary with critical commentary on individual aspects or common features of the genre being examined. Textual notes define what is difficult or obscure and emphasize literary qualities. Revision questions are set at appropriate points to test your ability to appreciate the pre-scribed book and to write accurately and relevantly about it.

In addition, each of these Notes includes a critical appreci-ation of the author's art. This covers such major elements as characterization, style, structure, setting and themes. Poems are examined technically – rhyme, rhythm, for instance. In fact, any important aspect of the prescribed work will be evaluated. The aim is to send you back to the text you are studying.

Each study aid concludes with a series of general questions which require a detailed knowledge of the book: some of these questions may invite comparison with other books, some will be suitable for coursework exercises, and some could be adapted to work you are doing on another book or books. Each study aid has been adapted to meet the needs of the current examination requirements. They provide a basic, in-dividual and imaginative response to the work being studied, and it is hoped that they will stimulate you to acquire dis-ciplined reading habits and critical fluency.

Graham Handley 1992

The author and his work

William Butler Yeats was born near Dublin in 1865, the son of the distinguished artist J. B. Yeats. Without some knowledge of his life a full understanding of the poet's work cannot be achieved: he once said, generalizing about 'the poet', 'His life is an experiment in living, and those who come after have a right to know it'. His own early life was indeed an experiment, with virtually no formal education. With a father largely absent in London and a mother content to listen to the folk-tales of local story-tellers, the young poet-to-be absorbed the history and mythology of Ireland from the tongues of the peasants of Sligo.

Yeats's very early education was brought to an abrupt halt when his father discovered that he was being taught to sing

> Little drops of water
> Like grains of sand,
> Make the mighty ocean
> And the pleasant land

Whether it was to the metrical arrangement of the lines, or the philosophy contained in them, that his father took exception we are not told, but the young Yeats was swiftly removed from that particular school.

In 1876 the family moved to London, and Yeats found himself enrolled in the Godolphin School at Hammersmith. With the freedom he had known in Ireland suddenly curtailed, he felt that he had been betrayed. There were, however, other and unusual compensations; being plunged among alien boys, he wrote, 'Presently I forget my troubles, absorbed in two things I had never known, companionship and enmity'. His grip on his Irishness intensified amid such opposition, and every holiday in Sligo increased the contrast in his mind between the two countries.

In 1880 the family returned to Ireland, and at the Erasmus High School, Dublin, in an atmosphere of purposeful noise, Yeats's education continued. ('I had not thought it possible that boys could work so hard . . . We read Shakespeare for the grammar exclusively.') Fortunately his father had introduced him at an early age to a wide range of literature, and this new teaching left unharmed his appreciation of both Blake and Shakespeare.

In 1884 Yeats became a pupil at the Metropolitan School of Art, Dublin. He had little special ability in drawing, and happily spent the bulk of his time doing what he most enjoyed – writing. Two years later his career as an artist was abandoned: he knew that he was a poet, and that was enough for him.

Yeats returned to London with his family in 1887, and from their home in Chiswick Park he met some of the great literary figures of the time – William Morris, George Bernard Shaw, W. E. Henley and Oscar Wilde. 1889 marked the publication of *The Wanderings of Oisin* (pronounced Usheen) and a number of other poems, and his first meeting with the lovely passionate revolutionary Maud Gonne. In 1892 he became a founding member of the Irish Literary Society.

1896 was a crucial year in his life; it was then that he met the wealthy artistic Lady Gregory and spent the first of many summers at her home, Coole Park, planning the Irish National Theatre. In that year too he first met Synge, in Paris. Shortly after, his mother suffered a stroke with resultant brain damage that led to her death in 1900.

The crisis year came in 1903, when Yeats lost his beloved Maud Gonne to Sean MacBride, a fellow-revolutionary, but 1905 saw the founding of the Abbey Theatre. In 1907 Yeats defended Synge at 'Playboy' riots in the Abbey Theatre, and in 1911 toured the USA with the Abbey Players. It was there that he met Ezra Pound, who was later to act as his secretary.

In 1916 the Easter Rising of the Irish Republican Brotherhood took place and between 3 and 9 May fifteen leaders were executed, among them Maud Gonne's husband: Yeats wrote 'Easter 1916'. In the following year he proposed to Maud Gonne's adopted daughter, Iseult, who rejected him. He then married Georgie Hyde-Lees, whom he had known for five years; and during their Sussex honeymoon, the new Mrs Yeats discovered a gift for automatic writing. In the same year his book of poems *The Wild Swans at Coole* was published.

With the outbreak of the Irish Civil War in 1922, Yeats accepted an invitation to become a member of the Irish Senate (roughly equivalent to our Second Chamber). In the following year he was awarded the Nobel Prize for Literature and he travelled to Sweden to accept the prize personally.

'Sailing to Byzantium' and 'Among School Children'

appeared in 1926, but in 1927 Yeats became seriously ill with congestion of the lungs and a general breakdown in health. In 1928 *The Tower* was published, followed in 1930 by *The Words on the Window Pane*. 1931 saw him awarded a DLitt degree by Oxford, and in that year he visited Lady Gregory at Coole for the last time before her death in 1932: *The Winding Stair and Other Poems* was published during that time. In 1936 he edited *The Oxford Book of Modern Verse*, and in 1938 saw his last book, *Last Poems*, through the press.

Yeats was suddenly taken ill on 26 January 1939, and died two days later; he was buried at Roquebrune in France. In 1948 his body was brought home to Ireland: at the funeral there was a military guard of honour, and the Government was represented by Mr Sean MacBride – Minister for External Affairs and Maud Gonne's son.

He was buried at Drumcliff 'under bare Ben Bulben's head', the stone inscribed as directed in 'Under Ben Bulben':

> No marble, no conventional phrase;
> On limestone quarried near the spot
> By his (the poet's) command these words are cut:
>
> *Cast a cold eye*
> *On life, on death.*
> *Horseman, pass by!*

The tributes were many, including one in verse by W. H. Auden in generous acknowledgement of Yeats's great influence on twentieth-century writing.

Critical introduction

Guideline to topics in the poetry of Yeats

1 *Yeats and symbolism*

In a story by Saki, 'The Jesting of Arlington Stringham', it is said of Lady Isabel, the progressive heroine: 'She slept in a hammock and understood Yeats's poems, but her family denied both stories.' And the fact that James Joyce considered Yeats, alone of his generation, to be a greater writer than himself also suggests that there is something special about Yeats's use of imagery and symbolism. The poet himself seems to be almost perverse about his readers' unravelling of the riddle of his meaning. He takes it at one remove from the elucidation of the symbol when he says, 'I have said several things to which only I have the key. The romance is for my readers. They must not even know there is a symbol anywhere. They will not find out.' In an age which insists on meaning in everything, a poet who thus clouds his thinking and expression will undoubtedly be at some disadvantage. Yet the use of symbols was for Yeats a kind of discipline as well. They were to be used to 'convey to others what could not otherwise be communicated'. The test of their effectiveness was to be 'the least possible amount of unintelligible matter' that was left.

It is not surprising that Yeats should have been attracted to the poetry of William Blake, and in an essay on that poet he says: 'A symbol is indeed the only expression of some invisible essence, a transparent lamp about a spiritual flame.' Reality for both these poets was to be found beyond straightforward prose meaning and sense. Indeed, one of his most revealing statements in this context was: 'Quite suddenly I lost the desire of describing outward things.'

It must be rememberd too that he always composed aloud, rather as Wordsworth often did, and so the sight of the lines on the page was of little help to him. It was on this count that his father (apologizing to Edward Dowden, Professor of English Literature at Trinity College, Dublin), said: 'His bad metres arise very much from his composing in a loud voice.' The poet himself, however, got his own back, perhaps unwittingly, by describing the professor as 'a man born to write the life of Southey'.

Yeats constantly spoke of the agony that metrical composition was for him: 'Nothing is done upon the first day, not one rhyme is in its place: and when at last the rhymes begin to come, the first rough draft of a six-line stanza takes the whole day.' Nor did he suffer any illusions about his poetry's effect on the reader. Sending some verses to a young girl, he said: 'I am afraid you will not much care for them, not being used to my peculiarities, which will never be done justice to until they have become classics and set for examinations.' Perhaps now that his work has attained that stage, we may find the reason for so many interpretations of both the man and his poetry.

We may leave to the poet himself the last word on the agony of composition and the effect he sought. He was always after the elusive impression of spontaneity:

> I said 'A line will take us hours maybe;
> Yet if it does not seem a moment's thought,
> Our stitching and unstitching has been nought.'

Clear proof indeed of his desire to achieve the art that conceals art.

2 *Ireland: the country and its politics*

I might have found more of Ireland if I'd written in Irish, but I have found a little, and I have found all myself.

It was to his native land that he first turned, to its myths and legends, for the subject matter of his early poems. As Louis Macniece says, 'Irish nationalism was a clumsy vehicle for Yeats's ideals, but it was a vehicle of sorts'. In the tales of Irish heroes that he retold, he found escape and a comfortable situation beyond reality. As he lacked any firm faith and the stability of a true religion, he created this for himself in myth and legend. In his *Autobiography* Yeats writes: 'I had made a new religion, almost an infallible church, of poetic tradition, of a fardel of stories.'

He turned this country of his into a dream land, a Celtic Utopia clearly divided into two groups, the peasant and the aristocracy. It was only when he turned to the latter for inspiration and came under the influence of Lady Gregory that the same kind of charges of betrayal made by Browning against Wordsworth in 'The Lost Leader' (i.e. 'Just for a handful of silver he left us . . .') came to be made against Yeats.

In 1909 he realized that his mind was dwelling 'more and more on ideas of class'. In fact he was totally absorbed with the theatre in the first decade of the century, and came close to Lady Gregory and her son Robert as they worked together on plans for a truly Irish theatre. This country mansion existence gave Yeats time for contemplation, and we see clearly what he found attractive in his comments on Coole Park, Lady Gregory's home. To the poet the idea of 'no compelled labour, no poverty-thwarted impulse' must have seemed totally suited to the artistic temperament. He saw no reason for such an idyllic existence to be threatened. In his life he always opposed violent revolution, though admiring the courage of the people. So he put in his plea for the continuance, and even support, of such a mode of life: 'How should the world be better if the wren's nest flourish and the eagle's house is scattered?' Such comments, however, have to be taken in the context of the time – not so long before Yeats wrote – of the great hunger, when some two million people, a quarter of her population, left famine-stricken Ireland.

When Yeats finally found Irish myth no longer sufficient to sustain his poetic impulse, he turned to himself and the defining of his own character, for his inspiration. This probably served to open his poetry to a wider public, since the English, at least, have always found Irish history, life and thought difficult to comprehend. Our education doesn't really encourage the acceptance of myth and legend as part of the fibre of our being. After Anglo-Saxon times and the Beowulf epic, our eyes turned to the Mediterranean and there found inspiration from legends that were not native to our shores and so could be treated more objectively.

Linked with the myth were the politics. 'It was through the old Fenian leader, John O'Leary, I found my theme.' The theme, of course, was Ireland. So the poet attaches himself to the Irish Republican Brotherhood and takes the oath, '. . . that I will do my utmost to establish the national independence of Ireland and that I will preserve inviolable the secrets of the organization'. The last part of the oath no doubt appealed to a paricular side of Yeats's nature.

Something of the poet's detachment from external events may be gathered from his almost completely ignoring the First World War (1914–18). The section of Irish society in which he moved was almost totally in favour of Ireland's entering the war against Germany. But for Yeats it was not Ireland's war; he was affected by it on a personal level only, as we find in the poems inspired by the death of Major Robert Gregory.

The conflict between Irish politics and the ruthless dedication of Maud Gonne to the cause of Irish freedom caused the love of his life to bring him great anguish and, ultimately, to founder.

3 Maud Gonne

It is impossible to estimate the effect on his writing of the poet's love for Maud Gonne. In her Yeats found the fusion of romantic and patriotic love; their relationship was to be stormy – 'I was twenty-three years old when the troubling of my life began' – but attraction to this woman was deep and instant: 'I had never thought to see in a living woman so great a beauty.' Sadly, however, from Yeats's point of view, Maud Gonne was no intellectual and had no taste for literature; for her his patriotic writings never went far enough. Even 'Easter 1916' did not entirely please her – there was not enough passion in it.

> Yet this lady
> took
> All till my youth was gone
> With scarce a pitying look.

However hard the poet fought the one-sided passion, with but small return from his loved one, yet it gave him an object. Maud Gonne acted like a catalyst to his inspiration: 'How much of the best that I have done and still do is but the attempt to explain myself to her? If she understood, I should lack reason for writing, and one can never have too many reasons for doing what is so laborious.' So his love for Maud Gonne gave a kind of compulsion to his work, almost a challenge to make himself understood to her.

We have only to look at *The Wind among the Reeds*, where we find the bulk of Yeats's lyrical verse in the symbolist manner, to have some feeling for the effect that this love had on the poet. The greater part of the book is given over to lyrics of rejected and frustrated love. The book is Maud Gonne's alone. Much later, Sean O'Casey spoke of her (at a meeting where he had to defend his having written critically of the Irish in *The Plough and the Stars*), in a much more realistic manner: 'She never seemed to have understood Yeats the poet. Indeed, she could not, having little of the poet in herself, so that she never felt the lure of melody.'

It would appear that Yeats had failed completely to make himself understood by this implacable woman, yet, whether he failed or not, the situation sparked off some of the finest of his poetry and gave him a starting-point from which he proceeded to his greatest work.

4 *Magic and the occult*

In the *Monthly Review* of 1901 there is an essay by Yeats entitled 'Magic', in which he states the following beliefs:

(a) That the borders of the mind are ever shifting, and that many minds can flow into one another, as it were, and create or reveal a single mind, a single energy.

(b) That the borders of our memories are as shifting, and that our memories are part of one great memory, the memory of Nature herself.

(c) That this great mind and great memory can be evolved by symbols.

When these ideas are transferred to poetic expression, we begin to understand the difficulties that beset the reader of Yeats's poetry. Link this with his interest in the occult, and we are in deep waters indeed. Names like Madame Blavatsky, quasi-religions such as Theosophy, and societies like the Dublin Hermetic Society, all give us cause to doubt whether we will be able to follow the workings of such a mind; or even whether, having uravelled the riddle, we will find the effort worth while. One thing, however, is certain, and that is that we cannot possibly ignore the influence of such ideas on the poet's work. Nor can we take much comfort from such critical statements of his work as:

Coldly received, his history is nonsense, his psychology is nonsense, and his explanation of life is nonsense too.

Yeats, however, had no such doubts about his own ability to explain the universe. About the ideas behind the founding of the Hermetic Society he says:

It was proposed that whatsoever the great poets had affirmed in their finest moments was the nearest we could come to an authoritative religion, and that their mythology and their spirits of water and wind were but literal truth.

No wonder the war generation, which needed the expression of something real in poetry, found that such ideas filled them with suspicion. But Yeats exulted in the knowledge, shared by few, that he had acquired from the reading of secret books. We can see now a little more clearly what he meant by the statement quoted earlier: 'I have said several things to which only I have the key.' It can surely be no coincidence that a fellow countryman, James Joyce, took very much the same attitude in prose as Yeats did in his poetry. The vast number of explanatory books on the work of each writer gives some indication of their success in concealing their meaning from the non-elect.

For Yeats, one of the most obvious attractions in the occult and esoteric societies was their concern with ritual and ceremony. It was the traditional and the ordered that had appealed to him in the aristocratic way of life. Signs and diagrams were meat and drink to his imagination, and they stimulated his deepest thinking. The image of the interlocking cones was his basic concept, and the word 'gyre' became his watchword:

Civilisation is narrow and intense, like the apex of a cone – but it gradually loses its impetus, broadens and so dissipates its energy.

Some critics, I. A. Richards for example, find the poet's signs and symbols merely irritating, and regard them as evidence that Yeats has used them simply as machinery to give some system to his philosophy:

Now, he (Yeats) turns to a world of phantasmagoria about which he is desperately uncertain. Mr Yeats takes certain feelings of conviction attached to certain visions as evidences for the thoughts which he supposes his visions to symbolize.

Here again, however, Yeats was convinced he was dealing with basic beliefs, and what really matters is that for him this was truth and a reality beyond sense. Probably of all our poets, Yeats is the one whose progress we can follow most clearly. He saw his own work as an architectural structure carefully designed and steadily developed. To the end of his life he arranged and re-arranged his poems so that this progression might be seen. Age, among all things, irritated him:

I am tired and in a rage at being old. I am all I ever was and much more, but an enemy has bound me and twisted me.

It is fitting that his last poem, meticulously prepared in September 1938, for whatever eventuality, should also be his own elegy, and end with his epitaph. 'Under Ben Bulben' brings his work to an ideal conclusion, though some find it too slight a vehicle for the summing-up of a lifetime in which, as Katharine Tynan said: 'He lived, breathed, ate, drank and slept poetry.'

Poem summaries and commentaries and textual notes

from Crossways (1889):

This group of poems represents the early work of Yeats; at this time he was still 'in the leading strings of poetry'. When he undertook revision of his work for definitive editions he tells us that he thought of leaving out most of them. As we have them, they are much rewritten and revised. The title of this cycle of poems originates from his idea that he was attmpting to follow 'many pathways'.

The Song of the Happy Shepherd

This poem must be seen as contrasting with the one that follows it here, and the obvious parallel in poetry is with Blake's *Songs of Innocence* and *Songs of Experience*. The tone of the first is, as befits a song, light and airy in octo-syllabic lines with alternate lines rhyming for the most part, though there are the occasional couplets. The theme of the poem is that 'words alone are certain good'. Structurally, it may be divided into three sections, and we might remember that it was called 'Song of the Last Arcadian' in one of Yeats's early collections. The first section – in effect a verse paragraph – deals with the belief that words, not facts, survive; that words record deeds, and that the earth itself may be merely a passing 'deed'. The second section covers the passing nature of things, and says that there is no point in searching for 'truth', except within oneself. This means ignoring the stars, which cannot be reached by man, and taking instead the sea-shell, which will echo the story told to it in reformed and lasting melody. In the last section the songs are for the 'hapless faun'; and the poem ends with the invocation to 'Dream, dream, for this is also sooth'. The poem is lyrical in tone, rightly consonant with the song of an Arcadian shepherd, and it is written in simple language but with the occasional superb coinage, like the double-barrelled 'echo-harbouring'. The expression is mature, with insistent alliteration, some archaisms (sooth), and it appears to be indebted to Spenser in terms of the Arcadian idea.

Arcady Arkadia, a mountainous region of Greece, traditionally known for the contented pastoral innocence of its people.

Grey Truth i.e. the search for it. The poem thus becomes an exercise in praise of the imaginative as distinct from the factual way of life.

Chronos One of the Titans, he succeeded Uranus as ruler of the universe, but was overthrown by his son Zeus. He reflects here time and change.

Word be-mockers Fine economical coinage to indicate the short span of the man of action who mocks words.

Rood The Cross.

sooth True.

the optic glass Jeffares rightly notes here an echo of Milton's 'optic glass' in relation to Galileo in *Paradise Lost* Book I, line 287.

star-bane Destruction, poison.

echo-harbouring i.e. which will contain your words and reword them in 'melodious guile'.

ruth Compassion.

faun i.e. Latin rural deity with horns and tail.

The Sad Shepherd

This poem is written in longer lines, to indicate a different mood. There is immediate personification; and a sense of isolation and loneliness is conveyed by the nature of the appeal, unanswered, to stars and sea. The parallelism with the first poem (and the fact that it is an exercise) can be seen here in the use of 'humming sands' for instance, as distinct from 'humming sea' in the first poem. The interested student might look for other instances, and see exactly how they affect the meaning and the emphasis in the poem concerned. A close look here too will show that the structure is experimental, for the poem has twenty-eight lines and is in effect two different-style sonnets (fourteen lines each) tacked together. Ultimately the sad shepherd comes to the shell, but instead of the variant rewording his song is changed to 'inarticulate moan'. Yeats has shown here both sides of the creative coin – words that last, and words that die and are forgotten. Both poems are thus a commentary on the poet and his writing: how words are vital and live; or how they disappear and are lost.

Sorrow Simple, conventional personification.

persecution of her glory i.e. as long as he is near the sea he is aware of its overpowering beauty that cannot be of help to him.

heavy story i.e. sad.
my ancient burden Long-felt melancholy.
the sad-dweller ... sea-ways lone The isolated shell.
wildering whirls Alliterative, but really 'bewildering' twists and
  turns.

Ephemera (things that are short-lived)

In this poem, originally sub-titled 'An Autumn Idyll', the poet
explores the fading of passion, in part in the form of a dialogue, with resultant dramatic force; the only hope for the
'lovers' is that they will have eternity in which to continue
their love, though line 21 introduces the idea of reincarnation.
The poem is written throughout in blank verse; it contains
natural personification (Passion), repetition and contrast of
the past and present, youth and age. The description is symbolic of the inevitability of age; the woods are 'round them',
the yellow leaves are 'like faint meteors' (note implication of
the loss of power), while the use of 'dead leaves' (symbolizing
dead physical love) in 'bosom and hair' is an ironic and
poignant contrast with the romantic excesses of youth where
maidens sometimes deck themselves with flowers. The man
then urges 'unrepining hours', and we return to the title of the
poem with the phrase 'a continual farewell', i.e. that change,
saying good-bye to the past, is permanent.

pendulous lids Hanging, drooping eyelids, indicating age,
  tiredness, a lack of liveliness.
worn Tired (us out), or even 'angered'.
like faint meteors The simile expresses colour, mood, even their
  'distance' from each other.
A rabbit old and lame A superb symbolic equivalent to the
  'death' of Passion seen in animal life.
Autumn was over him The liveliness he had known in the
  spring had departed.
other loves await us The hint is of reincarnation.
a continual farewell Change.

The Stolen Child

Yeats used an area in Sligo for the background to this poem.
The power of the fairies was particularly strong there, but the
human child, 'solemn-eyed', had yet to make some sacrifices
in its journey to the land of faery; everyday comfortable sights
and sounds had to be abandoned for a new and carefree land.

Yeats referred to his verse about this time as 'a flight into fairyland from the real world' and 'the cry of the heart against necessity'. The language is simple (again, we might almost say, in keeping with the subject); the tone is lyrical with a refrain that echoes the serious intention despite the lightness of the form. There is initially an echo of Christina Rossetti's 'Goblin Market', an economic richness of natural observation. But the theme carries an adult overtone, the life of imagination being cherished as distinct from the life of 'necessity'. The lyrical control, with varying length of line and ease of rhyme, is masterly.

Sleuth Wood This is between Lough Gill and Dromahair.
vats Tubs, barrels.
For the world's more full of weeping The essential sadness and suffering of life is in this refrain, which runs the length of the poem.
glosses Casts a glow over.
Rosses 'sea-dividing, sandy plain' in Sligo.
foot it i.e. dance.
Glen-Car A lake, north-west of Sligo.
bathe a star i.e. because the reflection would not be clear.
solemn-eyed i.e. with sleep, but perhaps already with the misery of the world.
the hob Side casing of fireplace, having its surface level with the top of the grate.
bob Dance, move up and down.
oatmeal-chest A store, the meal being used in the making of cakes and porridge.

Down by the Salley Gardens

This was Yeats's reconstruction of an old Irish song. The young man is too self-centred to take the advice of the maiden, and suffers as a consequence, though in one of the early versions on which Yeats based his poem the girl is fickle. This is therefore a finely economical condensation; it is too short to be a ballad, yet tells a story in which repetition, the use of nature and the simple language effectively combine to convey the universality of the experience: sadness and loss in love. The poem is a measure of Yeats's mastery of form even at this stage in his career (and allowing for revisions). In fact it is in eight lines of rhyming couplets. Note the exquisite balance which juxtaposes feet, hand; leaves, grass; and, most significantly, love, life.

salley Willow.
weirs Dams across the river.

The Ballad of Moll Magee

Yeats thought this poem too close to the popular ballad of the country, and apparently based it on a sermon he had heard preached at Howth. The pathetic story of the old woman, so exhausted that she 'lay' on her child in sleep, is in typical ballad form, i.e. four-lined verses with the second and fourth lines rhyming, told in the first person, with the local dialect giving it a kind of authenticity. It is imbued with compassion.

childer Archaic, still local, form for 'children'.
shore lines in the say Fishing lines running into the sea.
saltin' herrings i.e. those brought in by the local fishing fleet.
but weakly i.e. quite poor in health.
minded ... minded Note the ironic effect of the word in view of the coming accidental death.
Ye little childer dear The tone is made effective by the fact that she is addressing the *living* who are *dear* to someone, just as her child was dear to her.
red and pale Alternately angry and frightened of the consequences.
Kinsale In Cork, another fishing port.
boreen A narrow lane.
byre Cow-house.
Blowin' i.e. starting her fire by blowing on it, a further underlining of the poverty.
keenin' The crying chant of the mourner.
shinin' looks Again the stress on the fact that they are alive.

Revision Questions

1 Concentrate on *two* poems. By a close analysis of them, show how important the sense of place is to our appreciation of them.

2 Compare and contrast any *two* poems in which Yeats uses different verse forms.

from The Rose (1893):

In this section of his work Yeats made it clear that he was grouping his poems under three headings, personal, occult and Irish. The rose itself came to be a complex symbol for the poet, and was linked with the Rosicrucians and what he had learned of the occult in his connection with the rituals of the Golden Dawn. Obviously Maud Gonne too is embodied in the rose at times.

To the Rose upon the Rood of Time

The poet here pleads that he be allowed mystical understanding without having to forsake the world of reality with its own pleasures. Here the complex symbol of the rose represents spiritual beauty, eternal beauty and Ireland. In *Essays and Introductions*, Yeats wrote of 'tragic joy' that 'its red rose opens at the two beams of the cross, and at the trysting place of moral and immortal, time and eternity'. Thus this poem foreshadows a treatment of the great legends of the past, but its plea for the retention of an insight into reality as well as of mystical experience is a moving one. The poem is written in rhyming couplets which alternate between the lyrical, the rhetorical and the romantic in tone.

Cuchulain Hero of the Red Branch cycle of tales. (In the poem from which Yeats took the idea, the hero kills his son.)
wood-nurtured Note the fine economy of the double-barrelled word.
In all poor foolish things that live a day Note the compassion and humility in the tone.
rose-breath i.e. the inspiration towards mystical experience.
And learn to chaunt a tongue i.e. an underlining of the quality of mystical or occult communication.

Fergus and the Druid

The King here abandons his throne and the weight of responsibility for a more peaceful life in the woods. The poem takes the form of a dialogue in blank verse, the druid representing in Fergus's mind the attraction of life away from the court. He gives up his throne to Conchubar, son of his wife Ness by somebody else. The King here believes that he is abandoning 'my sorrow', but he has not really achieved this because, although he has won freedom, he can still 'feel the crown upon my head'.

Druid i.e. supposed to possess mystical, magical properties in communion with nature.

Red Branch kings These served the King of Ulster.

Conchubar King of all Ireland in the Red Branch period.

In the white border of the murmuring sea Superb descriptive flow, isolated, and in a sense conveying imprisonment within his kingdom by the use of the word 'border'.

Look on my thin grey hair The Druid puts the case against himself, playing a kind of pre-Christian devil's advocate.

Who wastes his blood i.e. gives himself up to the role he is supposed to play.

quern A primitive, hand-operated mill for grinding grain.

the small slate-coloured thing i.e. the bag of dreams.

Cuchulain's Fight with the Sea

Emer, Cuchulain's wife, hears from the messenger that her husband is bringing home a young concubine, Eithne Inguba. She sends her son to challenge the only other man who has taken the oath that he will reveal his name at swordpoint Cuchulain, who is the boy's father. The two meet as strangers and the son is slain. King Conchubar fears that his court will be overthrown in retaliation when Cuchulain wakes from his brooding state, and begs the Druids to cast a spell on Cuchulain that will turn his wrath against 'the invulnerable tide'. A fine narrative poem, the killing of the son by the father providing the basic narrative theme: for a much longer but stimulating parallel the student might look at Matthew Arnold's *Sohrab and Rustum* (1853). The control of the dialogue is dramatically effective: the poem is written in rhyming couplets which are rarely end-stopped but which flow with the mood of Emer's anger and the physical movements of the fight itself; they thus break continually with the emotional force. Above all, the poem tells a story with a fine control of mood, with a sense of the mystical and of fate, and with a marked pathos, centralized in the idea of father killing son.

raddling raiment in her dun Dyeing cloth red, in her hill fortress.

web i.e. that which is woven.

raddled Dyed red.

Has won the gold i.e. he is the greatest warrior and bringer of loot.

blench Turn pale.

sweet-throated i.e. Eithne Inguba.

It is not meet i.e. not fitting, not proper.

My father stands The son's recognition of his father's great power is ironic in view of what is to happen when he clashes with him.

Aged, worn out with wars Note the mother's cunning in cajoling her son into the fateful journey.

The Red Branch camp i.e. the army led by Conchubar.

the mournful wonder The sad concern, whether at his own guilt or for mystical reasons, or his sense of what fate has in store for him, we don't know – and this is part of the magic of Yeats's method.

the harp-string i.e. ballads sung in his honour.

After short fighting in the leafy shade Note how quickly Yeats gets to the combat – no words are wasted.

the dim sleepy ground i.e. death.

The dooms of men ... God's hidden place i.e. God keeps hidden the fate of his children.

Your head ... That I loved once A poignant recognition, for the son is like the mother Cuchulain once loved. But here the mighty hero is unaware of the connection, the realization in all its tragedy coming in the next few exchanges.

Cuchulain I i.e. the son's name, as well as his father's, though in earlier versions of the poem he was named as Finmole.

I put you from your pain Note the superb economy, the simple words to finish the terrible deed.

sweet-throated maid i.e. Eithne Inguba.

subtlest i.e. most cunning.

dreadful quietude Terrible silence.

Chaunt in his ear i.e. sing, intone false ideas (which he will act upon when he awakes).

to their mystery i.e. the mysteries (of magic, the occult), which they alone know.

horses ... cars of battles i.e. the waves, their noise and movement, set up in his mind the idea that they are his chariots and that he is fighting a battle.

invulnerable tide i.e. that cannot be wounded or defeated.

The Lake Isle of Innisfree

Here the poet dreams of escape to the idyllic island and the simple life. Innisfree is an island in Lough Gill, County Sligo. The poem was written in London, when Yeats described himself as 'very homesick', later asserting that it was 'my first lyric with anything in its rhythm of my own music'. He was to say, however, that the first line showed 'conventional archaism' and regretted the 'inversion in the last stanza'. He often expressed the desire for a solitary life, and the island was associated with Irish folk-legend.

I will arise A deliberate Biblical echo, the Prodigal Son (Luke 15, 18). Note that these three words begin the first and third verses; and that all three verses have alternate lines rhyming, but with a fine variation of the length of the lines, a rhythmic control and an intimacy of vision that make it a compelling, endearing anthology-piece.

wattles Interwoven twigs and branches forming the structure.

Nine bean-rows Nine is a mystical number but the lilting music of the phrase is the important thing here.

the bee-loud glade Superb evocation of sound, a contrast with the voices of men.

cricket sings ... linnet's wings Notice that the noises of nature are conducive to peace.

lake water lapping Natural onomatopoeic effect.

I hear it in Note the simplicity of the ending, a simplicity echoed in the descriptions of nature that precede it.

The Pity of Love

This poem, together with the three that follow it, were copied in a manuscript book and given to Maud Gonne. In this poem the activities of man (buying and selling), the weather, the lonely place 'Where mouse-grey waters are flowing', are all seen by the poet as threats to his loved one. The eight lines of the poem, with alternate lines rhyming, are thus a mystical encapsulation of the poet's uncertainty over his beloved. It is a sad lyric, very simply written, but with the one notable epithet quoted above, the individually coined 'mouse-grey'.

The Sorrow of Love

Three verses with alternate lines rhyming, the third verse being an ironic re-working, with subtle emphasis, of the first. The 'Helen' theme is introduced, and is present in the two poems that follow. It was Helen's love for Paris, and her abduction to Troy, that led to the siege by the Greeks, which lasted for ten years. In Yeats's own life, Helen is to be equated with Maud Gonne. The poem was much revised, and the first verse sets the pattern of contrast: here is the small fight (the sparrow) and the beauty of nature as distinct from man's own image, while the second verse focuses on Helen and the effect she had on history and on Yeats. The third verse marks the return to nature, and finds strife, sadness, the heavens devoid of beauty. The poem is the superb condensation of a mood:

love changes all (Helen and the noble Greeks and Trojans, as well as the poet in his contemplation of things).

red mournful lips There is a distinct transference here – the 'mournful' is descriptive of those she affected, and of the poet's sadness too.

Odysseus The subject of Homer's *Odyssey*, who took twenty years to return from Troy to Ithaca after the Trojan War.

Priam The last King of Troy, killed in the siege, and the father of Paris, the direct cause of the Trojan War.

A climbing moon ... an empty sky Indicates, it would seem, a love that his hopeless.

lamentation of the leaves i.e. evocative of sadness. Note too the identical line-endings of the first and third verses, which serve to link but also point the contrasting mood of this short poem's beginning and its ending.

Could but compose i.e. nature reflects the sadness of man, his conflicts and suffering.

When You Are Old

The expression here is marked by symmetry of form (as beautiful as the beloved), and it owes its inception to a sonnet by Ronsard (1578), the opening of which has been rendered into English (from the French) by Humbert Wolfe:

> When you are old, at evening candle-lit
> Beside the fire bending to your wool,
> Read out my verse and murmur, 'Ronsard writ
> This praise for me when I was beautiful'.

It will be apparent that Yeats is here indebted, but that his treatment is an individual one. It has been held by some that the initially endearing quality of the poem is replaced by a tincture of arrogance, for the beauty of the beloved has faded, and remains only in the poet's words. However, the superb focus comes with the term 'pilgrim soul', the implication being that only one man has loved the spiritual quality which informed her physical beauty. The third verse appears to mean that the poet 'fled' into the world of the imagination, losing himself in mysticism, speculation, with the loved one consigned to an old age consoled only by the memory of beauty and love. This is one interpretation, but there are obviously others of this controlled and tender poem, with its sadly ironic look into the future.

The White Birds

Again a poem in three verses, but this time in much longer lines, perhaps reflecting the birds in flight. It was written after Yeats's rejection by Maud Gonne, and after her assertion that if she could choose to be a bird her choice would be that of a seagull. The theme is one of weariness, but there are some arresting phrases and coinages and, throughout, a fine grasp of the rhythmic effects, a running alliteration and a visual flair.

the blue star The reference is to Venus. The time of day itself reflects sadness and weariness.

dew-dabbled Fine epithet in terms of the visual effect.

Danaan Fairy.

Time ... Sorrow So momentous is the experience to the poet, that the abstractions are deliberately personified to elevate the effect.

buoyed out on the foam As with Innisfree, the wish to escape from ordinary existence is implicit in this poem.

The Man who Dreamed of Faeryland

A poem written in four twelve-line verses with some variation of the rhymes within each verse, but regular in rhythm and effect. Each verse describes a part of the life-cycle; the first, the time of romance, which gives way to dreams of escape – to 'a woven world-forgotten isle' – dreams that mar the pleasure of the romantic experience. The second verse takes us into life much later, with its 'cares and fears', and once more the sight of something (this time 'bait') baits his imagination too, and it takes flight. In the third verse we find anger and mockery, but anger is forgotten in the contemplation of the 'knot-grass growing by the pool'. In each case it is something unpleasing which sets the mind off, and even in death he is tortured, for the worms give him no peace. It is a contained piece of symbolism, an expression of the frustrations of the life-cycle, the imagination being liberated by the things of the earth or the sea, into a 'faeryland' that cannot be lived, only sensed.

at Dromahair In County Leitrim.

some tenderness/Before earth took him i.e. some feeling of love or romance before he died.

woven world-forgotten isle i.e. faeryland, paradise, escape from worldly things.

Lissadell In Sligo.
money cares and fears i.e. poverty.
plashy Marshy, wet.
lug-worm A burrowing worm used as bait.
golden ... silver ... sun ... moon These repetitions in the
poem are aimed at creating the idea of perfection.
stayed his hungry foot i.e. delayed beginning to dance.
Scanavin In County Sligo.
unnecessary cruel voice i.e. because it disturbs him from the
present.
silver fret the gold Note the use again of these symbols.
Lugnagall The abyss referred to in Yeats's *Mythologies*.
vapour-turbaned Shrouded in mist, as a head is surrounded by
a turban.
spired i.e. wound themselves round.

The Two Trees

This poem is said to have been one of Maud Gonne's favour-
ites. The tree was a symbol much used by Yeats, for it has
roots in the earth, branches in the sky, and needs water to
nourish it. Here it is at first a beneficent symbol, offering life to
the beloved, but the other side of the image is shown as an
empty shadow of evil, and the mirror-image is not to be
trusted. The debt, as Frank Kermode points out, is to one of
Blake's *Songs of Innocence* ('Love And Harmony Combine').
This time the poet uses octosyllabic lines with alternate lines
rhyming; it is symbolic, difficult of simplistic interpretation.
But it is clearly divided into two parts: the first redolent of
good, the second of evil; the first of beauty and naturalness,
the second of temptation, of reflection rather than reality. A
close reading of the poem will indicate to the student where
the difficulties lie, but will also show the rich details of Yeats's
symbolic method. Sometimes complete comprehension of a
poem is not possible, but what we may get from it is a cast of
thought, the reflection of a mood or the deployment of an
esoteric language clear to the author but indicative rather
than clear to the reader.

The holy tree The tree of life.
dowered Given as a wedding gift.
a circle go Yeats's mystical conception, in which he saw the tree
of life as being made up of ten circles.
ignorant The emphasis here is that it is a virtue rather than a
fault.

Gyring Rotating, circling.
spiring A continuation of the tree trunk above the place where branching begins.
the bitter glass i.e. the mirror.
The ravens of unresting thought i.e. intellectual argument, restless mental activity.

To Ireland in the Coming Times

This poem binds together the ideas of the occult, the place of literature in the struggle for the independence of Ireland, and ends with a lone stanza to Maud Gonne. In the poem Yeats offers an apologia to those of his friends who found it difficult to follow the mingling of the occult imagery of the Rose with the Irish struggle. For Yeats, the symbolism had added a new dimension to his work, which consists of three verses of superbly controlled octosyllabic rhyming couplets.

rann A verse, part of a poem in Irish.
red-rose-bordered hem i.e. a coinage representing the occult, Ireland, Maud Gonne.
a measured quietude A period of peace.
My rhymes more than their rhyming tell i.e. his belief in the occult and the mystical which he wanted to fuse with the concept of nationalism.
elemental creatures Composed of the great forces of nature.
unmeasured mind That cannot be contained.
barter Exchange.
A Druid land i.e. having occult, mystical power.
benighted Intellectually or morally ignorant.
In truth's consuming ecstasy The enlightment given by full understanding.
For God goes by with white footfall Appears to mean that love, conventional religion, may pass him by because of his obsession with the occult and mystical, but in the next few lines he makes it clear that his love for her (Maud Gonne), his patriotism and his mysticism are interrelated.
Note: The men referred to are Thomas Davis (1814–45), leader of the Young Ireland Party, who founded the *Nation* in 1842; James Clarence Mangan, romantic poet and essayist (1809–49); and Sir Samuel Ferguson (1810–86), poet, antiquarian and translator.

Revision Questions

1 Write a detailed appreciation of any single poem in this section, bringing out clearly the meaning it has for you and, if possible, the meaning it had for Yeats.

2 Select any two of the poems in this section and show how they embody Yeats's mystical or occult beliefs.

from The Wind among the Reeds (1899):

By the time he reached this section of his work, Yeats had evolved a scheme of personalities both for himself and for those close to him. Through characters such as Aedh, Hanrahan or Michael Robartes he could deal with his own personality, which could be shared by all of them. This contributed to his lyrics an element of drama not dissimilar to that seen in the poetry of John Donne. There is much Irish material here too, and in the first poem this strain is much in evidence.

The Hosting of the Sidhe

This beautiful lyric is steeped in Irish legend and folklore, has short lines, a simple rhyme-scheme, and a refrain. It is finely descriptive, with an effective use of repetition.

Knocknarea In Sligo. Maeve, a great queen, is reputed to be buried there.
Clooth-na-Bare The old woman of Beare, who haunts many places.
Caoilte Companion of Finn and comrade of Oisin, he was a fast runner.
Niamh A beautiful woman belonging to the tribes of Dana. In a Fenian story she carried Oisin off for three hundred years.

The Lover Tells of the Rose in His Heart

The rose, which generally stands for perfection, is here threatened by the 'wrong of unshapely things'. To find the perfect beauty he desires, the poet feels that he must take himself away from others and build afresh. It is written in long rhythmic lines, for the poet finds it difficult to reconcile 'All things uncomely and broken' with his love, and the second verse deals with his wish to refashion things until they are consonant with his love. The rose image reflects once more both the personal and, beyond, Ireland.

your image i.e. the beloved's.

green knoll apart i.e. removed from everyday affairs, another island-escape equivalent.

The Host of the Air

In this poem Yeats transforms the old Gaelic folk-tale into a mystical ballad. The original told of a husband who heard of the keening of mourners as he returned to his home. They are keening for his own wife. The poem plays on the two ideas of joy and sadness, and the red wine and white bread have something of the communion ritual about them. O'Driscoll is lured by the fairies, the title of the poem referring directly to them; there is an enigmatic, mysterious quality about the whole poem, which has the effect of incantation and dream at the same time. Note too the repetition.

Hart Lake A lake in the Ox mountains.
The bread and the wine had a doom ... the host of air i.e. if you eat or drink faery food you are doomed.
A piper piping away Seems to represent the lure of the fairies, the temptation of the supernatural.

The Unappeasable Host

Here the Danaan children are the Gods of Ireland; in the ordinary imagination, the fairies. With the reference to 'candles at Mother Mary's feet' Yeats has interestingly incorporated Christian material into this poem.

ger-eagle A kind of vulture, the term formed on the analogy of gyr- or ger- falcon.
the North i.e. the wind.
O heart the winds have shaken The final lines stress the power of the Gods and the fact that they are more beautiful than the Virgin Mary – an indication of the grip exerted by folklore and superstition on the popular imagination.

The Song of Wandering Aengus

This poem was suggested by a Greek folk tale. The 'glimmering girl' was perhaps Maud Gonne. Yeats always carried in his mind the picture of his first sight of her, standing beside a bunch of apple-blossom. As always, there is the suggestion of a love that is unrequited. There is a fine lyrical note: moving and mystical, with the use of repetition and the fairy associations very strong indeed in terms of transformation and an experience beyond life.

hazel wand i.e. from the tree of life.
The silver apples ... the golden apples i.e. the symbols once again of perfection.

He Mourns for the Change that has Come upon Him and his Beloved, and Longs for the End of the World

In the original foreword to the poem, Yeats said that 'the boar without bristles is the ancient Celtic image of darkness which will at last destroy the world, as it destroys the sun at nightfall in the West'. Out of the folk tale-cum-legend heritage, Yeats has fashioned a love poem of positive sexuality and desire. The reaction is one of rejection of his own lust (the change that has come upon him) and the rejection too of the perpetual chase (to use his image) that is involved. This is yet another exercise in exploration of the feelings.

He Bids His Beloved be at Peace

The horses here are probably those that ruled over the country of the departed spirits: note the sensuality of the image of hair – an image much repeated in Yeats – and the equation of the four points of the compass with the moods and physical longing of man. There are, as ever, some fine descriptive touches and a sonorous rhythm that itself conveys the deep strong feeling of the poem. The last two lines are an invocation to tranquillity in love.

He Remembers Forgotten Beauty

This romantic evocation of times past plays again on the rose imagery, this time linked with the contrasting 'dew-cold lilies'. Technically this is one 24-line sentence, broken only by semi-colons. There is a superb handling of the octosyllabic couplets, a conscious dwelling on the various types of beauty recalled.

murderous moth Note the heavy alliteration, which indicates the power to destroy.
dew-cold lilies i.e. symbolic of purity.

He Gives His Beloved Certain Rhymes

In the first verse he refers to his use of myths and legends, while the second dwells on the language of poetry that romanticizes the beloved by comparison and exaltation. The language is exquisite, the balance achieved a fine one, and once again there is the sensual concern with hair.

The Cap and Bells

Of this Yeats says, 'I dreamed this story exactly as I have written it, and dreamed another long dream after it, trying to make out its meaning, and whether I was to write it in prose or verse.' The jester's cap and bells win the lady, but it is a 'flutter of flower-like hair' that has made his heart speak. It is a superb lyric, the blending of spiritual and sexual love set in a Blake-like enigmatic cast redolent of the highest artistry. Repetition, a kind of music, running alliteration, even narrative tension, are all present.

The Valley of the Black Pig

The poet's own note tells us that it is believed, according to a certain prophecy, that there will be a rout of the enemies of Ireland in a certain Valley of the Black Pig. According to Yeats, this is a common belief among the peasantry, and this poem is a short but measured utterance of the belief. It indicates Yeats's ability to handle yet another form.

cromlech A circle of upright stones or monoliths.
cairn Rough stones piled up as a memorial.

He Hears the Cry of the Sedge

This was written to Maud Gonne during a period of great suffering and sorrow. Yeats says that he made the ancient Tree of Life an axle-tree (shoulder- or cross-beam), 'for this was another ancient way of representing it'. The mournfulness and the mention of the sedge has a Keatsian echo, and certainly no birds sing in this brief, sad but lyrical reference to a legend.

The Secret Rose

Yeats believed that there would be a revelation when certain Celtic mysteries had been fulfilled. Here he uses a mixture of

Christian and pagan mythology: Conchubar is the 'king' who heard of the Crucifixion and reacted by chopping down a grove of trees, symbolic of the punishment he would have meted out to the Jews. Cuchulain met Fand. The man who drove out the Gods was Caoilte, and 'him who sold tillage' was a young man who appears in some West Irish folk tales. Again the superb control of the couplets, again the mystical invocation of the legends, again the personality of the poet identifying on a national and personal level.

inviolate Free from injury, unharmed.
in the wine-vat i.e. by drinking.
great leaves i.e. the Rosicrucian emblem.
Magi The wise men.
Emer Wife of Cuchulain.
liss Fort.
barrows Funeral mounds.
the proud dreaming king Fergus.
A woman of so shining loveliness i.e. the transference to the present has occurred – here this is a reference to Maud Gonne.

The Travail of Passion

The comparison of the suffering of love to the suffering of the Crucifixion, which is the central image of the poem. Again the image of the beloved's hair seems to be the only source of comfort. The poem is heavy with abandonment to suffering.

Kedron River crossed by Jesus on his way to and from Gethsemane.

He Wishes his Beloved were Dead

This is a development of an earlier poem, written to Maud Gonne when she was suffering from overstrain after famine relief work among peasants in Donegal. Death, he thinks, would keep his beloved with him always. The thirteen lines achieve the near-completeness of a sonnet: the imagery of the hair, the sun and moon as symbols make the poem typical of this period of Yeats's writing.

He wishes for the Cloths of Heaven

A dream-poem, a light-poem, eight lines of internal rhyme and an expansive lyrical tone – it is sentimental, romantic, self-pitying and yet at the same time exalted, for the dreams are the visions and the poems, the very stuff of which ecstatic love is made. There is an effective contrast between the first five lines and the last three, for these are in the conversational tone of self-depreciation, whereas what precedes them is poetic in the ornate sense of that word.

He Thinks of his Past Greatness When Part of the Constellations of Heaven

Another mystical poem, in which the lover remembers his past incarnations. He has been the tree of heaven on which the Pole Star and the Plough are hung, and he has, at the other extreme, been a rush trodden by the feet of horses. His great loss is the loss of physical love and the suffering this occasions him.

The Fiddler Of Dooney

This lively ballad is in sharp contrast to the rest of the poems in this section, and shows the poet's belief that salvation comes to the minstrel and the bard as well as to the religious and contemplative man. The tone is vigorous, a dancing measure, with repetition and refrain prominent; it is also a social and spiritual comment — happiness is a creed, perhaps the most important one to follow.

like a wave of the sea Perhaps an echo of *The Winter's Tale* Act IV, Scene 3: 'I wish you/A wave o' the sea.'
Peter By tradition St Peter sits by the gates of Paradise to welcome the spirits.

Revision Questions

1 By a close look at any two of the poems, show how Yeats uses particular themes in his work.
2 Write an appreciation, bringing out clearly its lyrical qualities, of *The Fiddler of Dooney*.

from In the Seven Woods (1904):

Five years divide this book from *The Wind among the Reeds*, and during this time Yeats had been much concerned with the spoken word from the stage. The poetry which followed was conversational in tone. The main theme of this section was the marriage of Maud Gonne.

The Arrow

Again, there is an association with Blake ('arrows of desire'), and a certain sexuality is evident. The poem is eight lines in rhyming couplets, and the apple blossom memory of Maud Gonne – Yeats's first meeting with her – also re-appears.

Never Give all the Heart

A cynical little poem in octosyllabic couplets, again with an echo of Blake, certainly autobiographical in tone and connected with Maud Gonne's marriage to Major John Mac-Bride in 1903. The theme deals with the loss of the poet, and the language is a simple expression of that grief but with a mask of cynicism.

Have given their hearts up to the play i.e. the enjoyment of acting their love rather than feeling it – the poet feels that he cannot act in this way.

Red Hanrahan's Song about Ireland

Yeats wrote a play, *Cathleen Ni Houlihan* (1902), in which Maud Gonne played the part of the old woman who represents a liberated Ireland. Here the five-line verses of the song have a sonorous, incantatory effect. There is a patriotic fervour inherent in the poem too, the refrain has a particularly musical effect, and there are the now familiar references to the lore and legends of Ireland.

Cummen Strand In Sligo.
left hand A reference to the superstition of ill-fortune.
like an old tree in a black wind The simile is a link with the mythology and the superstition.
Knocknarea Peak overlooking Sligo, with strong legendary associations.
Maeve The Queen of Connaught.
Holy Rood i.e. the Cross.

Under the Moon

Again the sonorous longer lines, this time evocative of depression, with a wide range of mythological and mystical reference.

Brycelinde A forest which witnessed the bewitching of Merlin.
Avalon The resting place of King Arthur in death.
Lancelot One of the most famous of the Knights of the Round Table. He was the lover of Arthur's queen, Guinevere.
Uladh The Irish for Ulster.
Naoise A warrior slain by Conchubar.
Land-under-Wave One of the names given to the underworld.
Land-of-the-Tower ... Wood-of-Wonders Part of Yeats's private language, and difficult of specific identification.
Branwen She was the daughter of Lyr: the second of the tales in the Welsh *Mabinogion* deals with her and her marriage.
Niamh and Laban and Fand For notes on the first and third see pages 29 and 33. Laban was Fand's sister.
dun Fortress.

O do not Love too Long

Simple ballad form, again evocative of depression or unhappiness in love. Undistinguished in tone; the repetition here (uncommon in Yeats), is almost bathetic. Again the cynical note, the feeling of being let down, is evident, but the reader is scarcely moved to sympathy.

so much at one i.e. close to one another in sympathy and feeling.
in a minute she changed Almost certainly a reference to the marriage of Maud Gonne and its sudden effect on the poet.

The Happy Townland

Yeats himself observed that this poem was an expression of striving after an ideal impossible of attainment. It is a finely sustained lyric expression of the quest for a paradise, and the symbols we have come to accept as a part of Yeats's method are markedly present. Read for the music, the magic of the incantation, the repetition, the dream: these are the dressings of the meaning, and the little red fox appears to be commenting on the fact that the search for paradise is the leaving of reality.

the townland i.e. perfection, the state of paradise.

golden and silver Symbolic again of the state of perfection, as we have seen earlier.

world's bane i.e. the destroyer of the world.

Michael A reference to the Archangel.

Gabriel In Yeats's mythology, Gabriel was connected with the Moon.

Revision Question

1 Indicate the part played by a personal idealism in any one or two poems in this section.

from The Green Helmet
and other poems (1910):

Between 1903 and 1910, when these poems were prepared for the press, Yeats continued the revision of his early work and remained heavily involved with the Abbey Theatre. The poems vary between those to Maud Gonne, still sounding the occasional poignant note, and those that look outwards to his life outside himself.

Words

The prose draft makes clear that the urge to write came from the desire to make Maud Gonne understand. Yeats also dwelt on the idea that if she had understood there would have been little point in his writing. Again there is an echo of Blake. The form is lyrical, four verses with alternate lines rhyming, a short poetic exercise in balance, for the two halves of the poem complement each other, built around the premise that (a) he wrote to make her understand and (b) he might have been better employed just living, experiencing life.

No Second Troy

This poem gives us – admittedly from a subjective standpoint – some idea of the kind of fanaticism possessed by Maud Gonne, who had always chided Yeats for not using his talents as an aid to political propaganda. The Helen–Maud Gonne duality is perpetuated through a number of questions that link the active anti-British idealism of the Irishwoman with the beauty of the legendary Helen. The title is thus ironic, the action of the poem imbued with a passion that is at once physical and idealistic.

most violent ways A reference to her activities, which involved engaging foreign help against the British.
courage equal to desire An expression of cynicism, of doubt.
tightened bow Again the Blake echo ('bow of burning gold . . . arrows of desire').
That is not natural . . . high and solitary and most stern i.e. Grecian qualities, underlining the Greek comparisons seeming always to be present in Yeats's mind in relation to Maud Gonne.
Was there another Troy for her to burn? Had Maud lived in Helen's time, instead of a 'most solitary and stern' present, could she not, too, have wielded as powerful an influence?

Reconciliation

Twelve-line poem in rhyming couplets, with the imagery ('deafened', 'blind', 'lightning') familiar now, since Yeats has used it before to describe his feelings at Maud Gonne's marriage. The poem is built around his reactions on the day he received the news that she was married, and the 'reconciliation' is the idealistic one of still cherishing his beloved in his imagination, to which he asks her to return to relieve his desolate state.

kings, Helmets i.e. what he was writing about when he heard the news.
pit Either the grave or the 'pit' in the theatre.
barren thoughts i.e. unproductive (because of her loss).

The Coming of Wisdom with Time

A balanced quatrain, written later than the foregoing (1909), the enigmatic association of nature and man being used as a symbol, the leaves being the past show, the root the permanence which may yield up the truth, is in fact the truth.

The Mask

The title itself is the image that was to become one of the poet's main themes, but the poem is a song from a play, with the parts clearly allocated to the man and the woman. He spoke of the mask as an 'emotional antithesis to all that comes out of their internal nature'. The first line is an immediate and dramatic echo of Blake's *Jerusalem*. The lyric form here is finely balanced in the dialogue, the outside/inside contrasts, the appearance/reality, passion/reason theme that informs it.

so there is but fire i.e. let's live for the moment (and not probe things deeply) – not bother to discover what is 'behind the mask'.

Upon a House Shake by the Land Agitation

The house is Lady Gregory's at Coole Park. Yeats never swerved from the idea behind the theme of the poem, i.e. that a leisured class ensured the continuity of culture. The argument is expressed in the form of a rhetorical question which runs through the alternately rhyming lines; we know the answer, but the imagery of the eagle and of wings is an extension of the idea of culture and in fact seeks to embrace the many worlds of the imagination open to those who can, by their way of life, afford to perpetuate what is best in life.

the lidless eye The eagle does not blink when it looks into direct light, like the sun.
eagle thoughts Echoes of Blake here, and remember Keats's stout Cortez had 'eagle' eyes.
Mean roof-trees The humble dwellings of the poor.
The gifts that govern men A reference to Lady Gregory's husband, a Colonial administrator.
Wrought of high laughter Reference to Lady Gregory's own writings.

At Galway Races

The sight of the racecourse and the horses gives rise to the thought that poets were once greatly attended to and commanded a following. The horsemen are connected with the poets as distinct from the 'merchant and the clerk': there is an obvious link in the 'race' of the imagination and its excitement. This is a light poem, but the implication is that poets will one day be listened to again.

hearteners among men Yeats would be moving in society at this time, and this is perhaps a reflection of the patronage he (a poet) was enjoying.

All Things can Tempt Me

This brief poem was written at Coole Park in 1908; it is a slight poetic exercise indicating how many things have lured him away from writing verse, like the beauty of a woman or the needs of his country. He also says how his views towards poetry have changed since he was young. There is an obvious reference to Maud Gonne, and an oblique reference to his managing of the Abbey Theatre.

Revision Question

1 What are the main themes of these poems? You may refer to any two or three in your answer.

from Responsibilities (1914):

These, with other poems, were published in 1916, and there is a wide range here, the rhetorical, his public, disillusionment, the giving up of the Celtic mystical 'trappings', references to his own ancestors.

Introductory Rhymes

This first poem is an account and defence of his ancestors, but there is a certain pathos as he confesses that his 'book' is a carrying on of the line, since he has no children. There is a wry humour in the performance too and pride in his inheritance, which is so mixed as to be in itself a legend.

free of the ten and four His ancestor was a Dublin linen merchant (Jervis Yeats), and the phrase means 'being excused some duties by the Parliament'.
Galway into Spain i.e. in the eighteenth century.
Old country scholar The poet's great-grandfather, the Rev. John Yeats. Emmet led the rebellion in 1803.
huckster's Trader's.
A Butler or an Armstrong The first an ancestor connected with a prominent family, the second one connected with a good military family.
Boyne The battle in which the Protestant William of Orange who succeeded to the English throne in 1688 defeated James II – a Catholic – in 1690. William is the 'Dutchman' referred to here.

Old merchant skipper Another ancestor from Sligo, a known smuggler but a brave man.

silent and fierce old man Yeats's maternal grandfather William Pollexfen of Sligo, a rather fearsome sea-captain and merchant.

a barren passion's sake Another reference to Maud Gonne and his unhappiness in love.

I have nothing but a book It was later to be remedied, but the pathos is very marked here.

The Grey Rock

The poet mingles the chat of the Rhymers' Club with the mythology of the Celtic gods meeting at Slievenamon. The theme of the poem is that Yeats has kept faith with his fellow poets. The poem is in octosyllabic lines with alternate lines rhyming, the tone is largely conversational, with recurrences to the poets from time to time as the link of the narrative. There are, of course, the usual personal references.

Cheshire Cheese An eating-house in Fleet Street. A number of poets and men of letters belonged to the club in the early 1890s, but the meetings of the Rhymers' Club were sometimes held in a private house of one of the members.

Goban The legendary mason.

Slievenamon In Tipperary, site of one of the palaces of the Celtic gods.

stirred his thews i.e. moved his muscles or sinews.

Hollo him on i.e. spur him in the chase.

a woman ... some poor lout The woman in the story is Aoife, but there is a strong indication that Yeats is once more mixing the personal with the legendary here, for he calls Maud Gonne's husband a lout, and the reference appears to be to her marriage too.

kept the Muses' sterner laws Remained true to the high poetic ideals (with which you had started).

Dowson and Johnson Members of the Rhymers' Club. The first (1867–1900), the second (1867–1902). Both drank heavily and were dissipated but were minor poets who made some reputation.

Rock-nurtured Aoife Fine epithet to indicate the toughness of this Queen of Scotland.

I have kept my faith i.e. with the poets of the Rhymers' Club.

the loud host before the sea Yeats has returned to the present, and with that there is a return to the personal too, an indication here, it seems, of his unpopularity with the nationalists.

To a Wealthy Man who Promised ...

Sir Hugh Lane had promised to give his collection of paintings to Dublin if they could be adequately accommodated. He was drowned in the *Lusitania*, but in a codicil to his will left the pictures to Dublin: because the will was incorrectly witnessed, Dublin did not get the pictures (and then only some of them), until 1959. Yeats cites patrons of Italian art in support of his own views. Again the poem is in short octosyllabic lines, with alternate lines rhyming, and there is a range of 'evidence' to show how Yeats felt. His own 'evidence' is of course cultural.

Paudeen's ... Biddy's i.e. the ordinary folk.
Duke Ercole A patron of the arts. His court was in Ferrara, which Yeats had visited in 1907.
mummers Actors or pantomimists, taking part in traditional folk festivals.
Plautus Roman dramatist, his plays were produced at the wedding of Alphonso, Duke Ercole's son, in 1502.
Guidobaldo Duke of Urbino.
That grammar school i.e. a reference to the superior accomplishments of his courtiers.
the shepherd's will Yeats is being ironic at the expense of the common people.
Cosimo A member of the Medici family who was exiled to Venice.
Michelozzo The architect who designed many buildings for Cosimo.
San Marco Library i.e. in Florence.
sucking at the dugs of Greece Taking intellectual nourishment from Greek culture, but 'dugs' is certainly earthy by Yeatsian standards.

September 1913

The occasion for this poem was a lock-out of strikers led by James Larkin, one of Lane's strongest supporters. Yeats is here speaking out against the kind of nationalism that is only interested in lining its pocket. In effect each of the eight-line verses consists of two quatrains, with alternate lines rhyming, and a refrain at the end of the verse that symbolizes the death, in the poet's mind, of the real ideals of nationalism. There is a strong identification with the heroes of his childhood in the mind of the poet, and a bitterness that things are not as they were, the opening invocation singling out the Catholic middle class as being responsible for the change.

O'Leary John O'Leary (1830–1907) had a great effect upon
Yeats, as we see from this poem. He spent fifteen years in exile
in Paris. He was one of the leaders of the Fenian movement.
the world like wind i.e. their fame is everywhere, it has spread.
the wild geese spread Irishmen fighting abroad, particularly in
France, Spain and Austria.
Edward Fitzgerald (1763–98) A romantic figure in the United
Irish Movement.
Robert Emmet (1778–1803) Led the 1803 rebellion, and was
executed.
Wolfe Tone (1763–98) Founder of the United Irish Club, died
in prison, by his own hand, in 1798.
'Some woman's yellow hair' i.e. Yeats's contemporaries don't
understand the greatness of the men of the past, and would
argue that they must have been in love to do what they did.

To a Shade

Here the ghost of Parnell is called from his grave to hear what
Ireland has done to the generous man who 'Had given their
children's children loftier thought'. Charles Stewart Parnell
(1846–91) was the great Irish leader brought down by a
combination of Gladstone and the Irish Church leaders after
his adultery with Kitty O'Shea had been publicized and
proven. There is a certain sardonic humour running throughout, but gradually this is usurped by the bitterness the poet
feels at the treatment of the modern benefactors of Ireland;
there is thus an ironic link with the Irish treatment of Parnell
in the past.

monument ... gaunt houses i.e. in Dublin.
In his full hands what i.e. the gift of the paintings (by Lane).
an old foul mouth Identified as William Murphy, proprietor of
two Dublin papers that opposed the Lane project; he had also
opposed Parnell.
Glasnevin coverlet A reference to the cemetery where Parnell
was buried.

The Three Hermits

Here the third hermit has already reached the state of grace
sought by the other two. His total indifference seems to be a
kind of triumph. The poem is not without humour, and the
short lines mask what is really a discussion of rebirth, one
contending that it is possible and beautiful, the other that the

change will be into a 'most fearful shape'. The tone is astringent, finely controlled, but there appears to be a sardonic comment even on the state of grace, which could merely be the reality of senility.

Beggar to Beggar Cried

The biographical background here may be significant, for Yeats felt that he was being inveigled into marriage by a lady somewhat past her first youth. The ballad-style form conceals a savage irony, which is present in the refrain. There is an earthy quality too, redolent of lust, necessity, reality, worldliness.

my pate is bare My head is bald.
that is between my thighs i.e. lust.
a devil in a looking-glass i.e. which will reveal how ugly she (or I) am.
barnacle-geese These are found in north-west Europe and Greenland. The hint is of noise – perhaps wanderlust or freedom – disturbing peace – conventional marriage.

The Mountain Tomb

The subject of the poem is Father Christian Rosencrux, who was supposed to have founded the Rosicrucian movement. Yeats is suggesting the futility of having an imagination not open to impressions, and the poem is symbolic of this thought. The first two verses underline the traditional, the celebration of what appears to be permanent and inviolable, but the last verse sounds the note of despair in 'In vain, in vain', for everything is buried.

onyx Pure jet black.

To a Child Dancing in the Wind

This was written to Maud Gonne's adopted daughter, Iseult. A superb lyrical moment of childhood seen in innocence before the onset of the worldly cares that have made the poet somewhat cynical.

Love lost as soon as won One is tempted to read for the autobiographical reference: Maud Gonne was married for only two years.

Friends

The three ladies referred to are Mrs Shakespear, with whom Yeats remained on friendly terms for some forty years; Lady Gregory, his patroness and friend, who offered hospitality at Coole Park, as well as advice about his personal affairs; and, finally, Maud Gonne. The form is lyrically light, a delightfully fluent and flowing poem. The tributes to the first two are almost lost in the rush of feeling that is not praise but anguish, an anguish and knowledge and 'sweetness' still there despite the poet's severance from his beloved.

eagle look The ability to stand off and view life from a distance.

The Cold Heaven

An attempt to trace the poet's feelings, associations and intensely subjective reactions when looking at the winter's sky. Twelve lines with alternate lines rhyming, the conveying of the mystical experience in which memory, loneliness, lust and the feeling of the movement of the soul are all present. There are some fine phrases: for example, 'rook-delighting heaven'. The poem is a searing experience, a touch of the unknown.

An Appointment

Yeats was temporarily alienated by the government because Sir Hugh Lane had not been given the post of curator of the Dublin Museum. It is a superb miniature with the natural order of things, as epitomized by the squirrel, seen as the corrective to the petty affairs of man. The lightness of touch reflects the movements of the squirrel and of the poet's mind as it responds both to nature and to the indignation he feels.

The Magi

This is the first suggestion we find in Yeats that the birth of Christ is only a partial revelation. The Magi are the 'pale unsatisfied ones', for even the Crucifixion is not, for them, the final revelation. The lines are harsh with dissatisfaction, but there is the usual fine imagery ('rain-beaten stones') and control of the alternately rhyming lines.

Calvary The place of Christ's crucifixion.

A Coat

This reflects the fact that Yeats has thrown off his former manner of writing and does not mean to return to it. The poem is a song itself, stripped bare, so to speak, to the melody; then damning his imitators, and looking forward to a clearer, purer utterance in the future.

Revision Questions

1 In what ways are these poems different from the preceding ones? Look at two or three poems in your answer.

2 Show how Yeats was influenced either by tradition or by public events in your analysis of any two poems in this section.

from The Wild Swans at Coole (1919):

Many changes had taken place in the poet's life before the publication of this section of his work; events had happened in the outside world which had influenced his writing, for he had again been rejected by Maud Gonne, and the Easter Rising of 1916 had taken place – which had led to the execution of Maud's husband.

The Wild Swans at Coole

Yeats considers the changes in his own life since his visit some nineteen years previously. The opening verse is superbly descriptive of the tranquillity of nature, the second with the movements of the birds perhaps paralleling the flight of the imagination. This sets up the train of reminiscence, then he focuses on the habits of the swans, the fine 'companionable streams' expressing the warmth he envies. This is further exemplified in the phrase 'their hearts have not grown old'. The last verse is a little enigmatic, but there is the terrible sensation of loss, almost as if the swans are passing away from his life to be enjoyed by others – perhaps a glance at the fact that youth and the experience of love have passed away too. The six-line verse with alternate lines rhyming, each verse climaxed by a couplet, have a mournful lyricism.

lover by lover Expressive of his envy of the swans who have mated, compared with the poet who hasn't mated with his beloved.

companionable Superbly evocative of warmth – again something the poet does not experience.

In Memory of Major Robert Gregory

This poem was inspired by the death of Lady Gregory's only son, killed in action over the Italian front early in 1918. Twelve eight-line verses, widely ranging in terms of reminiscence, after a lengthy introduction, but, focusing sharply on the human subject of the poet. The tone is finely conversational, but this does not preclude the use of elevated thought as the poem unwinds. The first two verses deal with the poet's home and the friends who have come to visit them; but the friends in the poet's mind at this time are the dead ones. The third verse is a direct reminiscence of the poet Lionel Johnson, while the fourth treats nobly and generously of the Irish playwright J. M. Synge. The fifth verse sees Yeats speaking of his maternal uncle, George Pollexfen, while the sixth marks his movement from these companions to the subject of the poem, Robert Gregory, whom he compares to Sir Philip Sidney. Thereafter the poem is devoted to memories and praise of Gregory's many-sided talents. It is a noble poem, full of wisdom and compassion.

fire of turf Peat-burning fire.

forgotten truth i.e. the interest in the occult.

A measureless consummation i.e. the achievement, all his learning and creativity successfully fused. The whole verse defines Johnson's attributes, though the 'falling' may simply refer to his reflexes when drunk.

John Synge (1871–1909) Author of *The Playboy of the Western World*. Yeats had met him in Paris, and greatly admired him.

a desolate stony place i.e. the Aran islands.

George Pollexfen The maternal uncle, greatly interested in signs, symbols, visions and astrology. To cap it all, he was a fitness fanatic and a hypochondriac at the same time.

square and trine The first means 'exact and correct', while trine means 'a third part of the zodiac', i.e. the aspect of two planets 120° apart.

to their lack of breath i.e. (I am used) to the fact that they are dead.

Sidney The parallel is not only on the score of talent, for Sir

Philip Sidney (1554–86), Elizabethan courtier-poet, died abroad, while still young.

The water-hen Note the unobtrusive natural observation with which the poem is infused.

a place ... meet i.e. a jump ... the hunt.

a great painter A reference to Gregory himself, whom Yeats considered very talented.

Soldier, scholar, horseman Note that this becomes a refrain in these three verses, which emphasize the subject's width of talent.

epitome In him all life was summed up.

What made us dream i.e. that he could live to be old.

took all my heart for speech A fine and moving statement, indicative of Yeats's own humanity.

An Irish Airman Foresees His Death

This poem, beautifully controlled and with alternate lines rhyming, sets forth the futility of war and is destructive of the idea of patriotism, since the airman is moved to fly by 'A lonely impulse of delight'. The poem thus captures the impetuosity of youth, which cannot wait for the future, and the past as something that has disappeared: life is the challenge of the present. But this summary does scant justice to a poem that embodies essential human truths in short compass: there is a universality about it. The language is terse, simple and direct; the fine balance of the poem is reflected in the balance of choice so carefully weighed by the airman himself. This balance is dependent upon running antitheses – hate, love, years to come, years behind, life, death: these give the poem a cynical overtone condemnatory of war. The repetition is a clever way of echoing the monotony life holds until one accepts a challenge.

I know Gregory.
that I guard i.e. the English.
Kiltartan Cross i.e. close to Coole.

To a Young Beauty

The poem is to Iseult Gonne, also courted by Yeats. It expresses disapproval of her wasting her time with a bohemian set. The first verse is light in tone, with the deliberate invocation of the song, but though the verse itself is finely chiselled, the tone becomes sharper and the ending is, as so often with Yeats, a superb transition to himself.

Ezekiel's cherubim ... Beauvarlet The comparison is with those mentioned in Ezekiel, often – here held up as the ideal – with those engraved or painted by Jacques Beauvarlet (1731–97), an inferior French painter and engraver.

Landor and Donne Obviously Yeats admired them both for their individual qualities. Landor (1775–1864), English writer and essayist, and John Donne (1572–1631), metaphysical poet who later became Dean of St Paul's.

To a Young Girl

The poem is addressed to Iseult Gonne; the subject quite simply is love, the poet claiming that his own experience of breaking his heart for Maud Gonne has at least given him the capacity to understand the feelings of a present-day fellow-sufferer.

The Scholars

Again a short, effective, ironic poetic exercise, built on the contrast that the passion that created art is reduced by the scholarly, academic activity around it. It is also an incisive comment on the aridity of old age, Catullus being used as the example of perpetual youth through his verses. The short six-line verses carry an epigrammatic terseness.

beauty's ignorant ear One is tempted to look for the autobiographical note here.

All Note the repetition, which reflects the hesitant movements, always the same, of age.

people think ... their neighbour knows i.e. the very limited areas of their scholarship.

Catullus The greatest lyric poet of ancient Italy (87–54 BC).

The Fisherman

A fine focus in short lines on the real and ideal, as the poet sees them. The poem is balanced on this contrast with telling economy, the first lines dealing with the ideal, the later with the real.

Connemara Tweed.

The dead man J. M. Synge, ideal representation of the simple life.

The craven There follows a list of the various aspects of human nature that represent the abject 'reality' of life for Yeats.

great Art Yet another reference to the controversy over the Lane
  gallery with which Yeats was so deeply involved.
under froth i.e. the misty rain.
down-turn i.e. fishing expertise.
cold ... passionate Note the contrast, inherent in the real and
  the ideal, perhaps even the two sides of man, which would come
  together in the ideal.

Her Praise

The poem is obviously about Maud Gonne and the fact that
she forsook public life to a large extent after her marriage. The
long lines seem to be a record of her activities among the poor,
and the poet's wish to hear them spoken of in appreciation.
Her devotion to the deprived in Dublin was well-known. The
poet unashamedly refers to the occasions when he has deliberately mentioned her name.

The People

A conversational poem, either imaginary or based on actuality,
of an exchange with Maud Gonne. It is thus in blank verse,
rather like dialogue in a play, and this gives it a certain
dramatic piquancy here.

this unmannerly town i.e. Dublin. Yeats is again referring to
  controversy.
most defamed i.e. slandered.
Ferrara Yeats is again thinking of the ideal age of patronage of
  the arts.
my phoenix A person of peerless beauty or excellence, here
  Maud Gonne.
and set upon me A reference to the fact that the audience had
  hissed her in the theatre after she had brought her action for
  separation against her husband.

Broken Dreams

This beautiful poem, with its subtle variation of long and
short lines – which give it both a contemplative and a lyrical
tone – is to Maud Gonne. It combines nostalgia with the
present, and is alternately elevated and conversational. Again
there is praise not only for Maud's beauty but also for her
activities, her public work; but here the obsessive is given
permanence and elevation.

gaffer An old fellow, an elderly rustic.

Burdensome beauty i.e. because of the cares it brings.

the poet stubborn Yeats is here referring to himself and his obsession for his subject – Maud Gonne.

in the grave Presumably a reference to the afterlife.

Your small hands were not beautiful Unusual emphasis, but the fact that they were not beautiful is a mark of her 'difference', here an endearing uniqueness.

Presences

A dream-cum-nightmare vision of a visit to his tower by three women. The first one is difficult of identification, but the 'child' is Iseult Gonne and the 'queen' is Maud Gonne. Even in this dream there is a reference to his own obsessive need to write about his 'unrequited love', and this gives the poem an ironic flavour.

Ego Dominus Tuus

Basically this is about the two sides of the human personality, that equated with the body, and that with the soul. The title is taken from Dante. The objective–subjective stances taken up in the dialogue can reflect the two sides of self, the mask and the reality. Apart from anything else – and there are mystical intepretations at the back of this – the first speech deals with 'magical shapes', and there appears to be in the ensuing exchanges a seeking for expression and for a full knowledge of self. Dante is said to have found himself, presumably through what he created, and the discussion on art leads to the assertion that it 'Is but a vision of reality'. The artists must have transcendent experiences, runs one argument, the opposite being the citing of Keats as the example of someone who created 'Luxuriant song' despite being 'poor, ailing and ignorant'. *Hic* (This one) replies by counselling 'imitation of the great masters', but *Ille* (That one) replies with the theory of his 'opposite' advanced at the beginning. The dialogue is logical, the conclusions somewhat obscure, and the poem is a fascinating example of self-dialectic. Again the dramatic quality of the blank verse is present.

Dante Alighieri (1265–1321) The great Italian poet who immortalized his love for Beatrice.

Lapo Possibly the son of the Ghibelline leader of Florence.

Guido i.e. Guido Cavalcanti (1230–1300) the Italian poet.

Bedouin's horse-hair roof i.e. the Arab and his tent.

The struggle of the fly in marmalade Superb domestic image (though from Verlaine) to contrast with the high-flown language of much of the dialogue.

Keats (1795–1821) The great English Romantic poet, who died of consumption at the age of twenty-five, perhaps best remembered for his immortal odes, particularly 'To a Nightingale'.

a livery-stable keeper Keats was the son of one, being born in Islington, though he was later apprenticed to a surgeon.

I seek an image From here until the end there is a degree of obscurity – the search for the opposite, the other self, the mysterious, the indefinable, the unknown – everything that goes beyond the ordinary.

The Phases of the Moon

This poem contains one of the main ideas of *A Vision*. The action is set in Yeats's tower in Thoor Ballylee, and he said of the poem that in it he endeavoured to explain his philosophy of life and death. Owen Aherne and Michael Robartes were the invented names of two of his friends. It is said that the poet formed his interest in 'The Phases of the Moon' and its 'mansions' from Chaucer. Once again the poem is a dialogue in the form of a debate over disagreement, together with the expression of ideas both logical and mystical, and is thus related closely to the previous poem. As befits the nature of the exchange, dramatic blank verse is again used.

Milton's Platonist ... the lonely light Samuel Palmer (1805–1881) illustrated the *Il Penseroso* of Milton. The illustration was called *The Lonely Tower*.

Shelley's visionary prince i.e. Prince Athanase.

Pater (1839–94) Famous for *Marius the Epicurean*. His style is ornate.

Twenty and eight The cycle, the patterns and the beliefs can be followed by a close study of this speech.

Athene takes Achilles by the hair A reference to *The Iliad* of Homer.

Hector is in the dust, Nietzsche is born The first one of the Trojan heroes, killed by Achilles, the second the German philosopher (1844–1900), founder of the creed of the survival of the fittest.

Sinai's top i.e. where Moses is supposed to have received the Ten Commandments.

the man within The dialogue is, of course, going on outside the tower, the 'man within' being the poet trying to solve the mysteries. There is thus a self-irony in these verses.

The burning bow that once could shoot an arrow Again the echo of Blake's *Jerusalem*.

The light in the tower window was put out Symbolic of the poet's finishing of the poem, and also of the fact that the debate of the moon's phases is over. For a full, though still complex, definition of so much that is at first sight obscure in this poem, the student is referred to Yeats's own work, *A Vision*.

The Cat and the Moon

Yeats himself wrote of the cat 'being disturbed by the moon, and in the changing pupils of its eyes seems to repeat the movement of the moon's changes'. He began to think of the cat as 'the normal man and of the moon as the opposite he seeks perpetually ...' This goes a long way towards explaining some of the obscurities here, but the poem is a fine lyrical expression of mystical response and association.

Minnaloushe This was the black cat that belonged to the Gonnes.

changing moon ... changing eyes Fine indication of reflection, of a mystic communion too between the great and small, the permanent and the animal, both of which are invested with mysterious powers.

The Double Vision of Michael Robartes

This poem is again the eye of the imagination involved with the phases of the moon. The four-line verses encapsulate the visions in a ballad, so that, though this is difficult of interpretation, it is a vividly and dramatically written one, the writer passing through the exhaustion of the experience and expressing symbolically its 'meaning' or associations.

Cashel In Tipperary, noted for its ruins.

A Sphinx The inscrutable statue of the desert, which looks on everything unchangingly, is here to be equated with the intellect.

A Buddha Apears to be the heart, or spiritual love, or both.

a girl at play i.e. expressive in her dancing of art and life, intellect and emotion.

at its fifteenth night This is the phase at which the body reaches a perfection impossible in life, pure soul.

Homer's Paragon i.e. Helen of Troy, but the use of the phrase
immediately suggests Maud Gonne, as does the tone of this third
section of the poem.
the burning town i.e. Troy.
Cormac's ruined house A reference to the fact that Cormac
McCarthy had restored the chapel there.

Revision Questions

1 Write an appreciation of the lyrical qualities of any *single*
poem from this group.

2 Write an acount of Yeats's feeling for the past in any *two*
poems.

3 How is Yeats's mysticism shown in any two or three poems
in this section?

4 Arguably, this section contains some of Yeats's greatest
work. Select any poem which you think is outstanding, and
show why you think this is so from close reference to the
text.

from Michael Robartes and the Dancer (1921):

Michael Robartes and the Dancer

The title poem is concerned with the breaking-off of the relationship between Yeats and Iseult Gonne, the he and she of
the poem representing the views of each. The dialogue is
concerned with art and the relative place of the soul and the
body. The poem, despite the dialogue form, has alternate lines
rhyming.

this altar-piece Obviously a representation of St George and the
Dragon.
Athene The daughter of Zeus.
Paul Veronese The Venetian painter (1525–88).
lagoon In Venice.
Michelangelo's Sistine roof i.e. the Sistine Chapel in Rome,
later described by Yeats as Michelangelo's 'fabulous'
ceiling.
Morning . . . Night Paintings in Florence.

Solomon and the Witch

A dialogue, this time between the poet and his wife, and dealing with the ideal union of lovers, with the poet as Solomon, alternate lines rhyming for the most part. The idea is that time can be suspended; it isn't, but the lovers will try again to achieve that perfect harmony where it is.

And this foul world were dead at last i.e. after the Fall.
an imagined image ... a real image i.e. the ideal as distinct from the reality.
the brigand apple i.e. the temptation fulfilled in the Garden of Eden.
spider's eye The female spider devours the male after mating.

Under Saturn

A poem apparently to his wife, but dealing with his present mood and the many associations of the past; alternate lines rhyming, the language is that of thought and contemplation, and consequently without any lyricism. It is personal without being intense; a piece of self-indulgence, which lacks the elevation of the poems that come before and after it.

saturnine Displaying a gloomy temperament.
lost love The inevitable reference to Maud Gonne.
the wisdom that you brought i.e. Mrs Yeats's own personal qualities.
Pollexfen See note, p. 47.
Middleton Another relative from the past.
a red-haired Yeats i.e. his grandfather.
I am thinking of a child's vow i.e. his promise in the distant past – and how he has broken it.

Easter 1916

Here the subtly varied short lines, with assonance and consonance and repetition, are a personal narrative of the Dublin rebellion of Easter 1916. The first part covers the poet's own recollections of the men who subsequently became martyrs, his casual acquaintance with them, his using them as foils for his own wit; but at the end of this section the line that is to become a refrain – 'A terrible beauty is born' – puts into perspective in a superb paradox the nature of their dying and the memory of their death. Friends, the 'young and beautiful'

Maud Gonne, and enemies are included in his survey in the second part of this moving and beautiful poem, which is alternately colloquial and elevated, as befits the facts and the idealism involved. The superb third part has the stone – permanence, Ireland, death – as its central symbol, and this is contrasted with a series of images involving changes in life. This symbol leads us into the fourth and final section, which becomes a debate in the poet's mind between the rights and wrongs of using personal feelings in a cause and thus becoming blind to human feeling in its immediacy and warmth.

them i.e. the rebels.

motley i.e. a traditional fool's parti-coloured dress. Used here, it is a cynical comment on life.

That woman's days Constance Gore-Booth, who took part in the Rising, and is the subject of two later poems.

harriers i.e. pack of hounds with huntsmen.

This man ... school Patrick Pearse.

winged horse A reference to Pegasus – here it may mean 'inspired them'.

This other Thomas MacDonagh, himself a dramatist and critic as well as something of a poet.

This other man ... lout i.e. Maud Gonne's husband, John MacBride.

the casual comedy Another cynical appraisal of the events.

Enchanted to a stone i.e. believed completely in the cause.

a stone of the heart This has been subtly led up to – the cause is seen as a permanent sacrifice. It also links with 'needless death'.

England may keep faith i.e. introduce the bill for Home Rule, which was in abeyance.

Connolly Trade unionist who was executed for his part in the revolt.

Wherever green is worn The national colour of Ireland, and hence synonymous with patriotism.

On a Political Prisoner

A poem about Constance Gore-Booth (see note on her in the previous poem) who became Countess Markievicz and who was at this time in Holloway Gaol for her part in the rising. The six-line verses strike a fine balance between the past and the present, between change and what was. The image of the bird acts as a running symbol of contrast with the prison: the gull of course indicates freedom.

Ben Bulben In Sligo (see 'Under Ben Bulben' later).
meet i.e. the hunt (remember the reference to the 'harriers' in 'Easter 1916').
rock-bred, sea-borne This enhances the contrast – she was then herself the symbol of a kind of freedom.
the hollows of the sea i.e. into which the bird could fall – as the subject of the poem did – into prison.

Towards Break of Day

This was a dream which Yeats and his wife had shared at the same time, the consonance between the dreams being the result of their having shared thoughts on the same theme. Aain there is the beautiful control, and a certain lightness of touch, as befits a dream that is, fundamentally, happy – and there is too the delight of its being shared.

The marvellous stag This, according to Malory in his *Morte d'Arthur*, suddenly manifested itself at the wedding feast of Arthur and Guinevere, pursued by dogs. There is obvious sexual symbolism here.

Demon and Beast

The principle of contrast, hatred here against desire, is central to this poem, but they give way to a sense of complete absorption and fulfilment in joy. The poet expresses the desire to extend the feeling in time, and thus to keep the two beasts at bay. The poem is in rhyming couplets.

perned in the gyre i.e. moved with a spinning motion. Yeats tells us that to him it meant the spool on which the thread was wound; 'gyre' similarly gives the idea of twisting.
Luke Wadding's portrait That of a monk.
Ormondes A distinguished family with whom Yeats was connected.
Strafford He was a statesman at the time of Charles I, and also Lord-Lieutenant of Ireland.
Could rouse my whole nature i.e. uplift me.
barren Thebaid Desert retreat of a number of early Christians.
Mareotic Sea Where early Christians practised self-denial.
Anthony Probably St Anthony of Egypt.
Caesars The verse deals with Egyptian monasticism, and since both Mark Antony and Julius Caesar – and later Octavius – fought in Egypt, this looks like an association of ideas.

The Second Coming

This poem speaks of the coming of a new spirit, and the image is of a brazen-winged beast which Yeats felt was always at hand but just outside his field of vision. The title is obviously derived from Christianity. It opens with an analogy, and the prophecy is a curious blending of Christian association with the bestial as the beast moves towards Bethlehem – perhaps as a terrible corrective to the world in which the poet finds himself. Obviously the Christian doctrine of Christ's second appearance on earth is the basis for the poem.

gyre See note above.
Mere anarchy Yeats was convinced that the world was in an evil state. Remember that this is written just after the First World War and while the excesses of the Russian revolution would be still in the mind.
Spiritus Mundi Spirit (or life) of the world.
Twenty centuries i.e. the span of Christianity.
a rocking cradle i.e. in the stable at Bethlehem.

A Prayer for My Daughter

Written to his daughter Anne, the poem has ten verses of eight lines each, of varying length, allowing, as so often in Yeats, of colloquial and elevated expression. The first verse describes the scene, refers to the sleeping child, and expresses foreboding. The second deals with the power of the wind and how the poet imagines that the future has come; while the third sees the beginning of the prayer proper, with the wish expressed that the child will not grow up so beautiful that she will lose the essential human qualities. The fourth verse uses history and mythology to show how beautiful women have behaved; while the fifth verse underlines the wish that the sleeping child will have a considerate nature. The sixth expands this into a contemplation of the quality of her thought, humour, and the hope of a settled existence. The seventh and eighth verses are given over to hatred, in particular intellectual hatred, which the poet condemns; while the ninth looks forward to happiness and a kind of innocence. The love of tradition is expressed in the final verse, with the hope that the woman's marriage will be rooted in 'custom and ceremony'.

the tower i.e. Yeats's own tower, where he lived.
murderous innocence A superb paradox.

Helen i.e. of Troy. And, of course, Maud Gonne and her
husband.
that great Queen Aphrodite, the goddess of Love in Greek
mythology.
bandy-legged smith Hephaestus.
Horn of Plenty Symbolic for 'anything you want', classical in
derivation.
Rooted in one dear i.e. settled into a fine tradition.
the linnet from the leaf A finely imaginative way of indicating
that harmony in nature is equivalent to harmony in the mind.
the loveliest woman born Yet another reference to Maud
Gonne; the lines which follow being a further (though repetitive)
commentary on her marriage.
rich horn ... laurel tree Note that Yeats returns to the two
images used earlier in the poem to indicate the importance of
fulfilment and harmony.

A Meditation in Time of War

A very brief attempt to convey the nature of a mystical experience, with the idea that God is the reality, mankind but a
dream.

Revision Questions

1 Write a Critical Analysis of either *Easter 1916* or *A Prayer
for my Daughter*.
2 Compare and contrast any two of Yeats's poems in this
section.

from The Tower (1928):

Yeats saw this as a bitter book, 'the best I have written'.

Sailing to Byzantium

This poem was written in 1926, and Yeats referred to it as a
poem 'about the state of my soul'. He knew much of the
Byzantine civilization through reading, and the poem is what
he called 'the search for the spiritual life through a journey to
that city'. Remember that it was written at the age of sixty-
one, and you will realize that it is a remarkable projection of

both the imagination and the intellect, with maturity of vision and an exquisite awareness of form. Again there is the fine balance between the colloquial and the elevated; and the four verses, the *ottava rima* (i.e. verses consisting of eight ten-syllabled lines, the first six rhyming alternately, then lines 7 and 8 rhyming together – as for example in Byron's *Don Juan*), are a condensation of wisdom, aesthetic appreciation and, above all, humanity and a degree of self-recognition.

That The reference is to the inadequacy of Ireland.

In one another's arms There is a certain poignancy here, of lost youth, and the following lines are evocative word-pictures of Ireland.

mackerel-crowded Superb double-barrelled coinage.

that sensual music i.e. living and loving.

Monuments of unageing i.e. great art that has survived.

Soul clap its hands The derivation may be from Blake, but the phrase itself is the arresting survival of the spirit as distinct from the flesh.

I have sailed the seas i.e. of the imagination, through study and the earlier visits to Palermo and Ravenna.

O sages The martyrs represented in a decoration.

perne in a gyre See note p. 57.

singing-masters i.e. inspire me.

artifice of eternity i.e. let me live through the spirit of art forever.

But such a form i.e. the identification of the soul with the finest in art rather than with the natural.

past, or passing, or to come Notice that it is the record in the finest art that survives time, unlike the 'begotten, born and dies'.

The Tower

In this superbly gossipy, egoistic yet sustainedly interesting poem Yeats deals primarily with himself – as ever – but also with persons associated by legend, story and tradition with the neighbourhood of Ballylee Castle. Varying length of line, alternate lines rhyming, and an emotive energy which belies his age – the contradiction of which has motivated him to write the poem – all cohere to make this an arresting poem.

Excited, passionate i.e. burst of creativity, response, imagination and insight – all are implied as we read on.

Ben Bulben See the poem on p. 90.

Plato and Plotinus The first the Greek philosopher (427–347 BC) and the second the Alexandrian philosopher (AD 207–270).

A sort of battered kettle A self-derogatory reference to his age.

like a sooty finger Note the fertility of the imagination.

Mrs French She lived at Peterswell some time in the eighteenth century. Yeats is merely repeating the legend, which carries a grotesque association of the inequalities of the distant past.

sconce i.e. a flat candlestick with a handle.

A peasant girl Mary Hines.

the man ... blind Anthony Raftery, a Gaelic poet who was, in fact, blind.

Homer Immediately the association with Helen and Maud Gonne is set up in the reader's mind.

moon and sunlight A re-invocation of the earlier imagery symbolizing perfection, completeness.

bawn A protected enclosure.

Whose images i.e. the ghosts.

The red man i.e. Hanrahan.

Old lecher Hanrahan.

Into the labyrinth of another's being i.e. transformed into the poet himself – Yeats – who is identifying with his own creation, and thus giving continuity to the traditions.

woman lost Inevitably, Maud Gonne.

It is time Note the sudden change in the verse form to the lyrical shorter line.

Burke ... Grattan The first the orator and philosopher born in Dublin (1729–97), the second the great Irish patriot and writer (1746–1820).

learned Italian things Evidenced in many of the poems in this selection are Yeats's affiliations with Italian culture, particularly in art and literature.

stones of Greece i.e. Greek sculpture.

Now shall I make my soul The whole of this last section is a moving and finely lyrical appreciation of what there is to lose in life, also of the finality of physical old age. The run-down into nature at the end masks the depth of the feeling. It is an extraordinary poem, the eye of the imagination as keen as ever, the poetic reflex more mature and compelling, and the form clearly expressed yet musical.

Meditations in Time of Civil War

Written at Thoor Ballylee during the disturbances of 1922 in Ireland. The seven poems here form a complete group.

I Ancestral Houses

The form here is *ottava rima* in five verses. It is a meditation on the nature of ancestral greatness: how it came into being;

and how it may be subject to change. The tone is initially conversational, but becomes more elevated as the poem progresses, the last two verses here ending with rhetorical questions.

Or servile shape i.e. life (in this kind of background) will not become subservient.
glittering jet i.e. joy in life.
but a mouse A comment on the decline, perhaps, of the nobility.
Juno Roman goddess, the wife of Jupiter.
But take our greatness i.e. greatness may require violence to preserve it.
escutcheoned i.e. shielded with armorial bearings.

II My House
The title refers to the tower. Change of verse form here into conversational intimacy, as befits the description of the interior and its associations.

the symbolic rose Here descriptive, but obviously charged with overtones.
stilted water-hen Fine descriptive term. A word-picture.
Il Penseroso's **Platonist** See note on Milton's Platonist, p. 52.
dwindling score i.e. his band of followers decreasing in number.
My bodily heirs i.e. his children.
Befitting emblems i.e. examples to act as stimulus.

III My Table
Sato's gift A Japanese sword.
Chaucer The great English author of *The Canterbury Tales* lived from 1340 to 1400.
only an aching heart Obviously a deeply held belief: witness the constant recurrence to Maud Gonne.
Juno's peacock screamed According to Yeats 'the last surrender, the irrational cry, revelation'.

IV My Descendants
a woman and a man i.e. his children Anne and Michael.
Through natural declension The following lines express natural parental concern for the children, but 'marriage with a fool' sounds the Maud Gonne marriage note yet again.
May build in the cracked masonry An image of desolation expressed – the loss of this ancestral house to his children if they should mislead their lives.
Primum Mobile i.e. prime source of motion or action.
an old neighbour's A reference to Lady Gregory.
a girl's love Presumably his wife.

their monument and mine An assertion of his belief in tradition.

V   The Road at my Door

Irregular i.e. Irish Republican Army, more commonly known today by its initials, the IRA.

Falstaffian i.e. Falstaff is a leading character in *Henry IV Parts I and II*, the bluff, witty, fat, idle, cowardly knight, friend to Prince Hal, later Henry V.

national uniform i.e. those loyal to the provisional government.

feathered balls of soot i.e. the chicks.

VI   The Stare's Nest by my Window

A starling built its nest by the poet's window at the time of the Civil War. It is an expression of his sense of the beauty of nature at a time of personal oppression and embitterment at the knowledge of the violence of the times. Note the reference to the incidents outside, which reflect his inward 'uncertainty'.

A barricade of stone or of wood A deliberate parallel with the starling's nest – the young soldier is the victim of human nature, just as the bees replace the birds that have gone.

VII   I See Phantoms of Hatred . . .

A fine change into a more sonorous verse, to mark the backward look into time and the associations set up by it. There is some superb natural description in the first verse and some detailed observation thereafter. Throughout, 'reveries perturb the mind', and the result is vivid, mystical, enigmatic, as so often in Yeats.

Jacques Molay Burned in 1314. Yeats tells us, 'A cry for vengeance because of the murder of the Grand Master of the Templars'.

Trooper belabouring trooper i.e. an image from the civil war.

Their legs long The whole verse is a brilliant visual focus – a reverie which is a series of word-pictures or paintings – the vision the poet is seeing at the time.

To brazen hawks These, according to Yeats, represent logic, but the visual vividness is still present.

The abstract joy Yeats is here underlining the continuity of his interests.

Nineteen Hundred and Nineteen

This poem, in six parts, was based on an account of atrocities – 'some horrors at Gort' – referred to by Lady Gregory in her journal. These were committed by auxiliaries and the notorious Black and Tans. Again *ottava rima* is the form employed.

1

An ancient image The sacred olive occurs in Herodotus.
Phidias Famous Athenian sculptor.
We had too many pretty toys A superb thinking back to his own earlier times (and those of Ireland) when all 'evil' always appeared to be in the past.
cannon ... ploughshare Appears to echo a verse in Isaiah.
a little powder burned i.e. unless there was some action, war.
dragon-ridden A direct reference to the atrocities mentioned in the brief introduction to this poem.
the world under a rule ... weasels in a hole Superb analogy – man equated with nature at the lowest level, and thus an ironic comment on the nature of man and his falseness.
Incendiary or bigot i.e. Yeats felt that Ireland was at the whim of the extremists: those who burned the big houses and those capable of extremist action without logic, merely with blind belief.
that stump on the Acropolis A reference back to the first verse, as this and the next two lines show.

2

Loie Fuller An American dancer.
Platonic Year Difficult of definition in brief compass, though the lines that follow carry their own interpretation.

3

Learn that we were crack-pated i.e. muddled, silly, to imagine (that everything inherently evil in the times could be put right).

4

The weasel's twist i.e. (we are proud) to be seen behaving like animals.

5

Come let us mock Note the cynicism here, the deliberate reversal of standards which violence has brought about and which is reflected in the tone being used.
Wind shrieked i.e. they disappeared.
Traffic in mockery The ultimate in cynical observation.

6

Here there is a return to the present and this is linked with some telling detail from the past.

Herodias' daughters The winds.
Robert Artisson An evil spirit of the fourteenth century.
Lady Kyteler An heretical sorceress of the fourteenth century.

The Wheel

Short, eight-line poem, alternate lines rhyming, dealing with the 'wheel' of the seasons, and with an underlying feeling that we are disturbed by the thought of death.

The New Faces

Another short poem, this time a delightful reminiscence of Lady Gregory and the past when she and the poet were young, is more real and vital than is the present day and those who now walk where they once walked.

catalpa From the 'gentle Pacific', a tree somewhat like an ash, but with outstandingly beautiful leaves.

Two Songs from a Play

These were written for Yeats's play *The Resurrection*. Here the poet sees a new era ushered in with the coming of Christianity; the songs are meant to be sung by a chorus of musicians.

1
a staring virgin An anticipation of the Virgin Mary, a direct link here with the Christian and the pagan.
Dionysus Killed by the Titans.
Muses i.e. the nine presiding over the Arts on Parnassus.
Magnus Annus Great year.
death but a play i.e. part of a cycle of birth and rebirth.
Another Troy See note, p. 25.
Argo's Made by the builder Argos – the Argonauts were the Greeks who set sail for Troy in the Argo.
the Roman Empire stood appalled Yeats's sense of historical perspective is asserting itself – the Empire was 'appalled' because ultimately it became Christian.
fierce virgin and her Star i.e. the Virgin Mary and the constellation Virgo. Yeats, as ever, sees the mystical connection of things.

2
Galilean turbulence i.e. Christ and his effect.
The Babylonian starlight brought i.e. the astronomers' prophecies of the reduction of man.

Doric The oldest of the four Greek orders of architecture, characterized by massive fluted columns without ornament.

Everything that man esteems i.e. joys in creating, even though what is created 'Endures a moment or a day'.

Leda and the Swan

This poem is about the rape of Leda by Zeus disguised as a swan. It is a sonnet, superb in its movement – physically evocative of the sexual thrust and power – and at the same time successfully merging the grotesque and the beautiful in the sweep of the wings. The immediacy, the visual quality, the rhetorical and probing questions that balance the physical probing, all these symbolize Yeats's superb control and organization here.

the strange heart i.e. of the swan and of the god.

A shudder in the loins i.e. sexual climax.

engenders there/The broken wall A reference to the birth of Helen, daughter of Leda and Zeus, and the sacking of Troy.

Agamemnon One of the Greek leaders in the siege, asassinated by Aegisthus and his own wife Clytemnestra, on his return from the war.

his knowledge i.e. his foresight, since he was a god.

the indifferent break Fine almost unobtrusive phrase to indicate that the god is satisfied, and has no feeling for her now.

Among School Children

The poem is based on a visit that Yeats, in his capacity as a senator, paid to a school in Waterford. Finely evocative of the present but more particularly and deeply of the past, with eight verses in *ottava rima*. The conversational opening gives rise to a number of associations, which the poet investigates through the mirror, so to speak, of memory.

cipher i.e. calculate.

be neat in everything This reflects the way the school was run.

public man See the note at the beginning of this poem.

Ledaean body Note a reference to the previous poem (perhaps ironically). But, as we see, also a memory of Maud Gonne.

Something of every paddler's heritage But there is something patronizing in the tone – as if none of these children could ever be equal to Maud Gonne!

my heart is driven wild In previous poems, Yeats has already expressed his increased capacity to *feel*; here we see how he is stirred by memory.

Quattrocento finger i.e. 15th-century art – Italian. Leonardo da Vinci.

pretty plumage He is thinking back to his own hair.

old scarecrow i.e. a deprecatory reference to himself; a term he also used in 'Sailing to Byzantium'.

spume Foam or froth.

paradigm Here it means essence.

Aristotle (385–322 BC) The great philosopher, teacher of Athens at its peak.

taws Thong for chastising.

Pythagoras Celebrated Greek philosopher who flourished between 540 and 500 BC.

Old clothes Again the scarecrow reference.

nuns and mothers i.e. the children being taught, and the nursing of the baby, are here in Yeats's mind.

O Presences A reference to the 'images' and the children.

Labour is blossoming The whole verse is difficult but appears to be about the *essence* of things rather than any particular manifestation.

Colonus' Praise

This is a translation of a chorus from the play by Sophocles, though Yeats himself did not read Greek.

Colonus Sophocles (497–405 BC) was born there.

Semele's lad Dionysus, son of Zeus and Semele.

Athene Greek goddess of wisdom. She was the patroness of Athens; and the olive was sacred to her.

Great Mother i.e. Demeter, earth-mother, sister of Zeus.

Cephisus A river.

Poseidon The sea-god.

Owen Aherne and His Dancers

A two-part poem about Yeats and Iseult Gonne, ironically written after his marriage, but dealing with the gap in years between the girl and himself, the name in the title 'masking' Yeats's own identity. Long contemplative lines in quatrains, with alternate lines rhyming. The last line in each verse is, in effect, a refrain.

Let the cage bird i.e. let like marry like, an underlining of the theme of the poem, which reflects the disparity of age.

O murderer i.e. his heart. Internal dialogue forms a major
aspect of the last part of the poem.
the woman at my side i.e. his wife.

A Man Young and Old

This is a selection from some eleven poems, and here each one
will be treated separately in terms of theme, technique and
any other characteristics worthy of note.

I   First Love
The reference is to Maud Gonne, the first in the series tracing
the development of his passion. Finely lyrical tone and, considering they were written when Yeats was sixty-one, remarkably fresh, vivid and clear, with a fine musical ear evident.

beauty's murderous brood A typically paradoxical association –
to be beautiful carries its own penalties.
maundering i.e acting listlessly.

III   The Mermaid
Brief poem, synopsis of a brief affair, though the lyric note is
successfully sustained.

VI   His Memories
This mixture retains the same form as hitherto.

cosseting i.e. spoiling, nursing, caring.
like the twisted thorn Perhaps a reference to the present, and
his age.
put all Troy to wreck This is another reference to the Helen/
Maud Gonne duality.

VIII   Summer and Spring
Lyrically descriptive of early closeness but with the sudden
switch into falseness; an enigmatic short poem, conversational
in tone.

IX   The Secrets of the Old
Like the previous poem in its enigmatic treatment of memory,
but here somewhat clearer because the supposed speaker is
hearing secrets; and one is tempted to identify – as in the
previous poem – the three people who are at the centre of it. It
strikes a rustic note quite deliberately, as if this is the 'mask'
the poet is assuming.

XI   From 'Oedipus at Colonus'
Complete change of verse form – appropriate to the elevation of
the subject – longer lines, which are in fact triplets of philosophical dignity, the kind of sentiment expressive of Greek tragedy.
The key line is the first, which advocates 'endurance' of what life
has to offer; then there is a tracing of the life-cycle, which ends
with 'The second best's a gay goodnight and quickly turn away.'
It is redolent of stoicism, acceptance of fate and adversity.

All Souls' Night

In this 'Epilogue', the three ghosts bring the message that the
truth will be revealed, provided there is no wavering of faith.
It was written in Oxford, and shows fine command of a
complex verse form and rhyming scheme in ten-line verses
with considerable variation in the length of line. The poet calls
up the 'ghosts' into his memory because of the significance of
the particular night.

Christ Church i.e. the Oxford College of that name.
muscatel Strong, sweet, white wine made from muscadines
  (muscat grapes).
wine-breath i.e. conjured up by the effects of drinking.
Horton One of Yeats's mystical friends. He died in 1919.
platonic love i.e. not partaking of sexual love.
Anodyne A medicine or drug able to assuage pain.
inclemency i.e. unkindness, bad weather (he longed for death
  because his beloved had died).
a slight companionable ghost i.e. the lady Horton had loved.
Florence Emery The actress Florence Farr, who died in 1916,
  and who had a long association with Yeats, having acted in *The
  Countess Cathleen*.
'minished i.e. diminished.
Among dark skins i.e. in Ceylon.
MacGregor The first name of another student of the occult, and
  friend of Yeats, who met him at the British Museum.
half knave i.e. no good.
mummy truths to tell i.e. presumably from the dead.
As mummmies in the mummy-cloth Note the repetition of the
  phrase, which indicates the twisting and turning nature of his
  thought on this All Souls' night.

Revision Questions

1 Write an appreciation of 'Sailing to Byzantium'. Do you
find it obscure? What does it tell us about Yeats?

2 In what ways does Yeats reveal his consciousness of age in some of these poems?

3 Which of Yeats's poems here do you find the most relaxed and why?

from The Winding Stair and other poems (1933):

In this section of his work Yeats returns to the reality of life, from the escape he had been seeking. A severe attack of influenza followed by congestion of the lung and a nervous breakdown gave him the realization that perhaps he was near to death. Such thoughts, as Swift suggests, tend to clarify our thinking. As he wrote to Mrs Shakespear once his hopes were again in the ascendant: 'I did not know how tired I was till this last blessed illness began, and now I dream of doing nothing but mystical philosophy and poetry.'

In Memory of Eva Gore-Booth and Con Markiewicz

The two sisters, the first dying in 1926 and the second a year later. The poem is a superbly lyrical recrudescence of their youth as remembered by the poet. The form is the octosyllabic line.

Lissadell The house in Sligo where they lived.
Conspiring among the ignorant She was politically active.
Utopia Written by Sir Thomas More, describing an imaginary island where all things, including the political organization, were perfect.
All the folly of a fight i.e. the rebellion, the civil war.
gazebo An ornamental look-out from which to view a particularly beautiful bit of landscape, as in a gentleman's estate – or over a river (as, for instance, that of the actor David Garrick, at Sunbury-on-Thames).

Death

Finely constructed short poem written about the assassination of a minister of the Irish Free State. It is antithetically balanced and expressed with both terseness and feeling.

Many times i.e. the idea of reincarnation is present here.
Man has created death i.e. made himself a sacrifice to it.

A Dialogue of Self and Soul

'I make my Japanese sword my symbol of life.' The location is obviously at Thoor Ballylee. The poem is in the form of a dialogue in eight-line verses, a deep pondering on the imagination of man, as symbolized by the priceless gift of the sword. The second part is given over to the idea that if life had to be lived again, with all its experiences, the poet would still welcome it.

Montashigi i.e. the maker of the sword.
fecund Prolific, fertile, probably here Yeats means of the imagination (from his unhappy love-affair all those years ago).
A proud woman Obviously a reference to Maud Gonne.

Blood and the Moon

The first verse in short lines, the following three in longer, representing the unravelling of the themes. 'Thoor Ballylee has a waste room at the top and the butterflies come in through the loopholes and die against the window-panes.' This suggested some of the imagery.

A powerful emblem up The tower.
Half dead at the top A reference to the incompleteness of the tower – and perhaps the poet had his own age ironically in mind too.
Babylon's A reference to the astronomers in Babylon.
Goldsmith Yeats is thinking of himself as a part of the great Anglo-Irish tradition of writers. Oliver Goldsmith (1728–74) author of *The Vicar of Wakefield* and *She Stoops to Conquer*; the Dean is Jonathan Swift (1667–1745), perhaps most celebrated for the daring satire of his *Gulliver's Travels*, Berkeley the philosopher (1684–1752). For Burke see note, p. 61.
sibylline Oracular, mysteriously prophetic.
farrow i.e. litters.
Saeva Indignatio Bitter anger, associated with the satire of Swift.

The Seven Sages

Linked to the previous poem, since again this deals with the great Irishmen of the past who were mentioned. The lines are broken up as befits dialogue, and are in blank verse.

Grattan's See note, p. 61.

pot-house i.e. public-house.

Oliver Goldsmith See note above.

the Bishop of Cloyne i.e. Bishop Berkeley. See note above.

Stella The lady to whom Swift was devoted, their friendship lasting throughout her life.

Whiggery Relating to the English political party, distant precursors of the Liberals.

saint ... drunkard The two extremes. Yeats is signalling his contempt for the middle-of-the-road view.

Burke's great melody i.e. his ideas and work for freedom (for example, of the American colonies).

what he had seen i.e. of the decline of agricultural life in 'The Deserted Village'.

trefoil Three-leaved. It appears to be a symbol of civil strife, as in Ireland.

They understood Perhaps they learnt, with humility, from common life.

Coole Park 1929

Yeats left a prose account of the plan of the poem. A beautiful poem in *ottava rima* which describes the house and its associations, it has the vividness of a painting and a superb and sustained identification with nature.

an aged woman i.e. Lady Gregory, the friend, writer and dramatist who had shared so much with the poet.

Hyde Douglas Hyde (1860–1949), first president of Eire, a poet and scholar too.

one that ruffled Yeats himself.

John Synge See note, p. 47.

Shawe-Taylor The nephew of Lady Gregory.

Hugh Lane See note, p. 42.

a woman's powerful character i.e. Lady Gregory's.

withershins Anti-clockwise, the reverse of normal.

are gone The house was later pulled down.

that laurelled head A testimony to her cultural, artistic activity.

Coole Park and Ballylee 1931

The now familiar *ottava rima*, here used tellingly and poignantly in praise of a beautiful place and its passing. The tone changes, being contemplative, philosophical, sardonic, and having a certain wisdom too. The first verse conversationally notes nature, while in verse two the poet, saddened at the thought of change, stands and watches a 'mounting' swan. He is drawn to the lake, however, and the poem appears to be balanced between the water and the swan, symbols of the life-giving force, perhaps, and the life of the imagination. Verse four is a simple recollection of associations, but verse five again broods on change, this time outside the house. The final verse deplores the passing of tradition, of a set way of life.

'dark' Raftery's i.e. a reference to the blind Gaelic poet. See p. 61.
demesne Landed property, estate.
tragic buskin The high, thick-soled boot worn by actors in Athenian tragedy.
rant's i.e. the acting, rhetoric of nature.
murdered with a spot of ink i.e. its colour could be changed.
that toils from chair to chair A reference to Lady Gregory.
a last inheritor A poignant reference to the death of Robert Gregory.
that high horse Pegasus.

Swift's Epitaph

Six brief, telling lines, ending with the assertion that Swift 'Served human liberty'.

At Algeciras – a Meditation upon Death

The poem is just what its title indicates, but it moves from the mixture of beauty and foulness of this particular place in Spain to reminiscences of childhood when the same subject took his mind. It is beautifully written. The contemplation is contained in the scene; then, as so often in Yeats, there is a return to the mind and to his past. There are three verses of six lines each, ending in a couplet.

Newton's metaphor Newton felt that he had spent his life gathering shells but had not penetrated to the heart of things.
Rosse's level shore In Sligo.
the Great Questioner i.e. God.

The Choice

A brief, eight-lined verse originally tacked on to 'Coole Park and Ballylee'. The straight choice, the poet believes, is in devoting oneself to life or to work: but when all is said and done, poverty, vanity or regret is what is left.

Byzantium

Complex poem, written in the eight-line verse but with a deliberately controlled length of line to vary the tone. The first verse has noble and sordid associations covering the span of physical life; the second deals with the spirit ('I call it death-in-life and life-in-death'). The third focuses on the singing of birds, and has pagan and Christian overtones; the fourth marks the return of the spirit of the dead to Byzantium, and their transportation, on the backs of dolphins, to Paradise. The ghosts are presumably those which created the great Byzantine art Yeats so revered.

unpurged i.e. still impure.
The fury and the mire i.e. anger and filth, the sordid.
Hades' bobbin i.e. a spirit returned from the dead.
death-in-life and life-in-death An echo of Coleridge's *The Ancient Mariner* ('The Nightmare Life-in-death was she').
changeless metal i.e. carved and thus permanent as distinct from the living birds.
of mire or blood This echoes the comment above, and takes us back to the first stanza of the poem. We are thus dealing with art, the supernatural, and man, the three covering the spectrum of experience.
the Emperor's pavement The forum of Constantine.
flames begotten of flame i.e. purified into immortality.
mire and blood Note again the echo.
Fresh images beget i.e. that set up fresh associations, fresh creativity.

The Mother of God

Three verses of five lines each, symbolic of the responses of the Virgin Mary to the miracle: the first verse carrying the associations of a painting; the second dealing with her supposed common life; the third with her contemplation of the actual miracle and the disquiet/wonder that she feels.

a fallen flare The effect is of a painting representing that, according to Yeats, 'She received the word through the ear'. Obviously the 'wings' are the wings of the angel.
tread the clothes i.e. wash them.

bids my hair stand up i.e. fear and wonder at what has hapened.

Vacillation

This fine philosophical poem, imbued with feeling, associations, self-examination, regret, is written in a variety of verse forms, which approximate to the individual moods. Each section is looked at separately here.

1 Simple short lines, considering the path of life 'Between extremities', but asking 'What is joy?'

antimonies Conflicts of authorities or laws.

2 The verse on the tree, one half being in flames; one half in green leaf. Both halves are beautiful.

Attis' image Attis, a god, who castrated himself.

3 This refers back to the first section, and in part answers its final question: get everything that you can for yourself, and then ponder on wife and family demands. The second section is more elevated, the poet urging 'preparation for your death', though this may mean in his case consciously working towards immortality through his verse.

Lethean i.e. from Lethe, the river of oblivion.
extravagance of breath i.e. recognize what you have done that is ephemeral, passing, not of any worth.

4 This describes briefly the mystical ecstasy he suddenly experienced in the London bookshop.

blazed Note the immediate connection with the tree of section 2.

5 This section is in complete contrast – natural beauty of scene forces him almost by contrast to recall things said or done (or not said or done) in the past, and 'Responsibility so weighs me down'.

In storm-scattered intricacy A superb visual image.

6 The theme of this section is 'Let all things pass away'.

Chou i.e. a member of that dynasty.
Babylon or Nineveh The first the great city of the East classed among the seven wonders of the world, the second the capital of ancient Assyria.

7 Brief dialogue between the Soul and the Heart. It leads to 8, in which he debates the theories of Von Hugel as expressed in his *The Mystical Elements of Religion*. Basically, a discussion here between Homer's and Christianity's ideas, Yeats being for Homer.

Isaiah's coal A reference to Isaiah's being touched on the mouth by a live piece of coal and thus purified.
simplicity ... salvation The contrast here is between the earthly and the life of the soul, the central debate of the last sections.
Saint Teresa i.e. the saint of Avila.
Homer is my example This looks back to 'original sin', and of course takes in the *Odyssey* and the *Iliad*.
The lion and the honeycomb This is a reference to Judges, 14.

Remorse for Intemperate Speech

Brief poem in short lines which is self-explanatory and which contains the usual subjective looking-back to the past.

that school i.e. my youthful associates.
fit audience i.e. people in sympathy with me.
Great hatred, little room Finely economical contrast: geographical, moral, spiritual limitations all implied.

Revision Questions

1 'Nostalgia is the key to Yeats's greatest verse.' Discuss this with reference to any poem or poems in this section.
2 Compare 'Byzantium' with 'Sailing to Byzantium'. What have they got in common and where do they differ?

from Words for Music Perhaps:

'I want them to be all emotion and all impersonal.'
'Sexual abstinence fed their fire – I was ill and yet full of desire.'

Crazy Jane on God

Four six-line verses with a refrain line at the end of each. The series probably derives from an old lady who lived near Lady Gregory. The brief story concerns her lover and his coming and going; the memory of a battle; the burning of an old ruined house; then another recurrence to the lover who has used her 'like a road/That men pass over'. It is really a short ballad.

Crazy Jane Talks with the Bishop

Every kind of experience, however extreme, is necessary for the understanding of life, just as 'fair and foul' complement each other in Shakespeare's *Macbeth*. Of course Crazy Jane reminds one of the witches in *Macbeth*, but her view of life is redolent of sanity and reality, however unpalatable the language. This is a fine earthy poem, well ahead of its time in its outspokenness and its appraisal of essential truth.

Crazy Jane Grown Old Looks at the Dancers

Based on a dream of the poet's about a dangerous dance that he associated with Blake's 'sexual love is founded on spiritual hate'. The refrain is, 'Love is like the lion's tooth', i.e. destructive.

thraneen i.e. cared not at all.
So that I had limbs A poignant recall and wish for the passion of youth.

His Bargain

The lover writes of how he has made a choice that transcends the decrees of fate. It is a short lyrical-cum-philosophical love poem.

Plato's spindle A concept of the fates from *The Republic*, with complex ideas, against which Yeats takes issue here.
Dan and Jerry Lout i.e. commonplace, fickle love is behind the choice of names.
A bargain with that hair i.e. Yeats is combining the image of the thread, fate, with the real image, the hair of the beloved, to which he will be true.

Lullaby

This superb lyric, written at the age of sixty-four, shows Yeats's mastery of the form and his imaginative and associative capacity at the same time. It might be compared with the

'Lullaby' ('Lay your sleeping head my love') of W. H. Auden. It is in three six-line verses, steeped in reference, wise and tender.

Paris The lover of Helen of Troy; he brought her there, and the Greeks began the ten-years siege as a result.

Tristram Here the son of the King of Lyonesse in Malory's *Morte d'Arthur*.

Eurotas River in Sparta.

the holy bird i.e. Zeus.

Leda The wife of the King of Sparta raped by Zeus, by whom she had Helen of Troy.

After Long Silence

Brief poem on the theme of age and youth, with the paradox that a decrepit body brings wisdom, whereas youth is love and ignorance.

Mad as the Mist and Snow

He is writing about how 'great genius' appeared to him when he was ill, and the poem is thus an expression of weariness with wisdom or the intellectual life. Three six-line verses, with the refrain.

Tully's open page A reference to Cicero (106–43 BC), master orator, philosopher and stylist.

'I am of Ireland'

Yeats derived this from a 14th-century song. It is in effect a ballad of a young girl dancing, inviting others to dance with her. One man responds, but finds many excuses not to dance with her, so that the poem becomes in effect a subtle allegory, updated, of the state of Ireland, its limitations, its triviality, and of how time (the refrain) has always overtaken it. The girl goes on singing and asking, deaf to what is said, an oblique and ironic commentary on the blindness of idealism.

outlandish gear grotesque garb.

The fiddlers are all thumbs The first of the phrases that indicates something rotten in the state of Ireland.

Old Tom Again

The thoughts of another invented character. The imagery of

sailing, building, storms, birth and death is descriptive of one's journey through life.

The Delphic Oracle upon Plotinus

The oracle of Delphi, fount of all wisdom, has been asked where the soul of Plotinus has gone. This is the reply in two superbly balanced six-lined verses.

Plotinus The Neoplatonic philosopher (AD 205–270).
Rhadamanthus One of the judges of those entering the underworld.
Salt blood i.e. life.
Minos Another judge of the underworld entrants.
Pythagoras See note, p. 67.

Revision Questions

1 What lyrical qualities does Yeats display in these poems?
2 By a close look at any two poems, say what you find either difficult or unusual about them.

from A Woman Young and Old:

Here we follow the life of a woman from childhood onwards.

I Father and Child
Written to his daughter, after she had praised the looks of someone she knew. A superb capturing of the difference between age and youth, and the temporary (or perhaps long-term) suffering this brings.

II Before the World Was Made
She is searching for the created pattern of herself. Again, a fine lyrical note is struck. The poem is about the essence of things, including, importantly in the second verse, the essence of love. The 'mask' theme is important here.

IV Her Triumph
This is the triumph of love after the 'casual improvisation' of love, the superficial being replaced by the wonderful experi-

ence of fulfilment. The 'dragon' motif of an earlier poem is used; out of mockery a true love has grown.

Saint George Again a reminiscence of a painting in Dublin, as we saw from 'Michael Robartes and the Dancer'.
pagan Perseus Remember that he slew the Gorgon, using his shield as a mirror to prevent his being turned to stone.
strange bird A reflection of the elevated moment.

V Consolation
The theme, as the title indicates, is comfort: despite being born there is comfort in the knowledge of love.

VI Chosen
This poem deals with destiny, the verse form being derived from John Donne.

the whirling Zodiac This marks the progress of the sun.
Scarce did he The verse is rich in sensual and cosmic description reflective of passionate love. It is also a reflection of astrological destiny.
the miraculous stream This is the Milky Way.
his heart my heart did seem Donne would have used the term 'soul', but it shows how Yeats was influenced by association in verse-usage with the great metaphysical poet.

VII Parting
Lyrical poem in the form of a dialogue at dawn: the theme of parting; the dawn of reality; the lady delaying her lover with the further temptations of love.

declivities Downward slopes – a sexual and cosmic image.

VIII Her Vision in the Wood
Here the lady gives herself a ritual wound. She is trying to recapture the distant past of youth and love, and after she has injured herself she sees a wounded man borne past on a litter (probably Adonis, killed by the boar). She finds herself caught up in the lamentation of the procession and then, in a moment of searing insight, realizes that the body is that of the lover whose 'lip' she has craved.

the string The harp.
Quattrocento Fifteenth century as period in Italian art.
Mantegna's thought i.e. the painter (1431–1506).

IX   A Last Confession

The movement is towards the final union of souls, but not before an honest examination of the pleasures of physical love and the withholding of the soul this involved. Ballad-form poem of fine lightness of touch. There is a strong metaphysical flavour about it, reminiscent of Donne or even of Marvell.

X   From the 'Antigone'

Again from Sophocles. Death is the final conqueror. Love and beauty must fade, though there is a bitter sweetness about such an ending.

Parnassus A mountain in central Greece, the centre of artistic and poetic activity.

Empyrean The highest heaven, supposed by the ancients to contain the element of fire.

Oedipus' child Antigone was the daughter of Oedipus, King of Thebes. She was condemned to be buried alive for covering her dead brother's body with earth, though forbidden to do so by Creon, who was then King. Creon's son kills himself out of love for Antigone.

from A Full Moon in March (1935):

Parnell's Funeral

The putting together of certain extracts from a lecture he had given in America; a superbly sonorous first part balanced by the second part, which is really colloquial.

Part I

the Great Comedian The great Irish leader Daniel O'Connell (1775–1847), who succeeded in obtaining Catholic emancipation in 1929, was particularly disliked by Yeats.

a brighter star shoots down i.e. a star is supposed to have fallen just as Parnell was buried.

the Cretan barb Based on a dream Yeats had of a beautiful naked woman shooting at a star. The whole of the next verse is given over to a complex extension of this, the priestess shooting a child who is to be sacrificed. This leads to the resurrection of Apollo. The 'Great Mother' is stamped on coins (fifth century BC in Crete).

Hysterica passio From *King Lear* – the onset of sheer madness.

when we devoured his heart i.e. as in the sacrifice of a god.

I thirst for accusation Note the complete change of tone.
the rhyme rats hear Almost certainly a reference to the
transmigration of souls.

Part II
de Valera Prominent Sinn Fein Leader. He became President of
Eire in 1959.
Cosgrave A Sinn Fein M.P. and leader.
O'Duffy Head of Irish police in the Irish Free State, disliked by
Yeats because of his Fascist tendencies.
Jonathan Swift See note, p. 71.

A Prayer for Old Age

It is obvious from the opening lines that this is a poem against
the purely intellectual in poetry, a defence of feeling. He likes
to think of himself as a 'foolish, passionate man'.

Supernatural Songs

These contain a linking of all Yeats's much used imagery –
loops, coils, circles and gyres. Yeats called the hermit Ribh 'an
imaginary critic of St Patrick'.

I Ribh at the Tomb of Baile and Aillinn
The opening is an invocation to the reader to listen to the
hermit's story. Baile and Aillinn had been 'transfigured to
pure substance'. They were Irish lovers who had died of
broken hearts, each believing the other dead. In death, in the
'light that lies in a circle on the grass', they achieve harmony.

IV There
This is the state of complete harmony, as the images in this
brief verse indicate.

V Ribh considers Christian Love insufficient
Here the hermit tells how he pursues hatred rather than love,
since it is 'a passion in my own control'. The theme here thus
is that by expressing the extreme at least some communication
with God will be established.

besom Kind of broom, bundle of tied twigs.

VIII Whence had they come?
What is the secret, the mystery behind the manifestation of
human love? What is it that drives people to particular action?

These are the questions the poem asks but to which it provides no answers.

Dramatis Personae List of characters.
Flagellant One who scourges or flogs himself.
Charlemagne King of the Franks, the great emperor of the West (742–814).

IX   The Four Ages of Man

They reflect the four stages of growing, from childhood, then the loss of innocence, the onset of thought, the spiritual element, each equated by Yeats with instinct, passion, thought, the soul.

XII   Meru

The title is from the mountain Kailas, where meditation by Indian mystics occurred. The poem is a comment on the self-destruction of civilizations by the men who have created them. Although civilization is an 'illusion', man's wars are a striving for 'reality'

Egypt ... Greece ... Rome i.e. symbols of past civilization.
Everest The mountain (scaled in 1953) in the Himalayas.

Revision Questions on the two previous sections

1 In what ways do these poems differ from Yeats's earlier verses?

2 Pick out a distinctive use of either symbol or theme in these poems and show how it contributes to our appreciation of them.

from Last Poems (1936–1939):

When he reached his previous group of poems, Yeats felt keenly that time was running out and that his grand design would not be completed. His rejuvenating operation gave him a fresh burst of creative energy, and he toiled feverishly to complete his work.

The Gyres

Again *ottava rima*, and using the familiar central image but here reinforced by Yeats's acknowledged 'love of proud and lonely things'.

Old Rocky Face Probably the hermit Jew of Shelley's *Hellas*.
  After a temporary brooding on the loss of the past, the poet
  advocates rejoicing at the coming of a new circle or gyre.
Empedocles The Greek philosopher, subject of a poem by
  Matthew Arnold.
a light in Troy i.e. the burning of the city.
Out of a cavern comes a voice i.e. the cycle of greatness is
  beginning again.
horses and women i.e. beautiful things – symbols that the cycle
  is beginning again.

Lapis Lazuli

Yeats had a piece of the deep-blue mineral. Here he dwells on the impending destruction of civilization. There is a certain affinity with the 'Ode on a Grecian Urn' by Keats; both poets are contemplating works of art and refer to what is implied as well as what is depicted.

Aeroplane and Zeppelin Memories of the First World War
  (1914–18) and the bombing raids; though the Zeppelin, thought
  to be a threat, proved useless.
King Billy bomb-balls A reference to William of Orange and
  the Battle of the Boyne.
Hamlet, ... Lear, Ophelia, ... Cordelia References to *Hamlet*
  and *King Lear*, Shakesperian tragedies.
Hamlet and Lear are gay ... An odd phrase, but Yeats means
  that their vision was 'enlarged'.
Callimachus Greek architect.
Two Chinamen This is the lapis lazuli, and the rest of the poem
  is devoted to description and imaginative association with it.

An Acre of Grass

Written in 1936, four six-line verses, deceptively simple in form and execution, with a couplet rounding off each verse, and variations in rhyme and consonance throughout. It is an assertion of faith in an 'old man's eagle mind', a faith that he will 'remake' himself in the image of those who were great in the past.

Timon (Of Athens) in Shakespeare's play of that name.
Lear Shakespeare's *King Lear*.
William Blake Poet, painter, mystic (1757–1827).
Michelangelo (1475–1564) Italian painter and sculptor who
worked on the ceiling of the Sistine chapel in Rome.

What Then?

Yeats thought of this poem as 'melancholy'. This suggests that
the feelings expressed in it are autobiographical, for the refrain line repeats non-achievement until the last verse. It
appears to be a comment on life, that whatever is achieved can
only be seen in relation to what could *still* be achieved in the
future – unless one is beset by age.

A small old house i.e. his own, Riversdale.

Beautiful Lofty Things

Brief nostalgic poem, beautifully indicating the nature of
Yeats's detailed and selective recall. The long blank-verse
lines are almost like the declamation of an old actor.

Abbey stage i.e. the Abbey theatre in Dublin, where Yeats
worked for a time.
'Saints ... plaster Saints' Obviously mocking.
Standish O'Grady (1846–1928) A novelist and historian who
exerted a great influence on Irish literature.
Augusta Gregory Her life was at one time threatened in the
civil war, during the burning of old houses.
Pallas Athene See notes, pp. 54, 67.
Olympians i.e. the Greek Gods.

The Curse of Cromwell

Cromwell's severity in Ireland is well known, and Yeats calls
him 'the Lenin of his day'. The Spartan fable is of the boy who
allowed the stolen fox to devour him rather than acknowledge
the theft. A cynical refrain runs throughout, acting as a comment on the times and on the passage of time at one and the
same moment.

Cromwell Oliver Cromwell (1599–1658), Lord Protector of
England and Ireland during the Commonwealth.
As the fox See the introduction to this poem.
I came on a great house This is a moving record of change,

recalling Coole Park; destruction; the coming of age; and the final cynical statement indicates that he feels he can talk to animals but not to people.

Come Gather Round me, Parnellites

A fine rhetorical ballad story of the Parnell tragedy, showing the usual ear for music.

Parnellites Those who continued to support Parnell after the news of his affair with Kitty O'Shea was made public. The characteristics of Parnell are accurately, romantically stressed – his Parliamentary responsibility and, in particular, his pride.
The Bishops and the Party i.e. the Catholic Bishops, who condemned Parnell, and the Party, who were divided against him.
A husband that had sold his wife A reference to Mrs O'Shea's husband, who had ceased to live with her well before the scandal became public.

The Wild Old Wicked Man

A poem involving a degree of self-mockery over his own idea of travelling. The first part of the poem deals with old age, but there is a constant interaction between the old man and God. The second part is given over to recollection of youth, the old man having been rejected by the lady in favour of religion. It is a light-hearted poem.

warty lads According to Yeats, peasants believed that warts were evidence of sexual power.

The Great Day

Cynical little poem about the unchanging nature of revolution throughout time.

The Spur

A semi-humorous quatrain upon his lust in old age – endearing because he can laugh at himself.

The Pilgrim

Five verses of four lines, followed by a refrain, which trace a passage through life. It appears to be symbolic of life and death, but the tone is ironic.

stations i.e. of the Cross.
A great big ragged bird appeared It seems to be symbolic of unspecified evil.
For I can put the whole lot down Perhaps a way of saying that he has acquired some wisdom.

The Municipal Gallery Revisited

Yeats considered this was one of his best poems – a superb reminiscence and at the same time a tour of the portraits in disciplined, finely controlled and structured *ottava rima*.

An ambush The first of the pictures mentioned. From now on the list begins, with personal anecdote and reminiscence accompanying it.
Casement Sir Roger Casement (1864–1916), member of Sinn Fein, tried to procure German aid, was tried for high treason, and executed.
Griffith Newspaper editor; he attacked Synge.
Augusta Gregory's son i.e. Robert Gregory, the subject of a poem by Yeats, as we have seen.
'onlie begetter' This phrase occurs in the dedication to the 1609 quarto edition of Shakespeare's Sonnets. Sonnets by other writers were included in the edition.
Rembrandt Renowned Dutch painter (1606–69).
that woman, in that household i.e. Lady Gregory.
No fox can foul Apparently derived from Spenser (1552–99).
Antaus-like He fought Hercules, but touched the earth to gain strength, his mother being Earth.
noble ... beggar i.e. expressive of both.
rooted i.e. in Aran.
I had such friends A generous tribute.

Are You Content?

Another poem that looks back on Yeats's ancestors, with whom we are now familiar. Three eight-line verses. The poet says that he is not content with what he has achieved.

He that in Sligo A reference to John Yeats (1774–1846).
That red-headed rector i.e. his son.
Sandymount Corbets A reference to Sandymount Castle, bought by Robert Corbet.
Robert Browning The poet (1812–89).

The Statues

A poem based on the idea that Pythagoras prepared the way for Greek sculpture, but after that the range of the poem is a wide one.

plummet-measured Calculated, having balanced lineaments.
Salamis The battle (480 BC) in which the Athenian fleet defeated the Persians.
Grimalkin A cat.
Pearse ... Cuchulain See note, p. 21.
The lineaments Return to a correct proportion, sense of perspective about art and life.

News for the Delphic Oracle

This is a light-hearted comment on one of the Lane pictures, Poussin's *The Marriage of Peleus and Thetis*.

codgers The gods seen as 'old fools'.
Niamh See note, p. 29. Yeats is using the Gaelic immortals too.
Oisin Hero of a long poem inspired by Gaelic legends.
Plotinus See note, p. 60.
Peleus on Thetis The picture in the National Gallery of Ireland.
Pan Goat-man, personification of nature in Greek mythology.
satyrs Half-goat, half-man.

Long-legged Fly

Fine historical association, the great events seen against the smallest thing, the fly. Eight-line verses, conversational in tone, followed in each case by the refrain of the fly in thought upon the stream. The second verse, by recalling Marlowe's lines upon Helen, invokes Troy and, inevitably, Maud Gonne in childhood. She, like the fly, is absorbed; the third verse describes the absorption of Michelangelo at work upon the Sistine Chapel. There is a fine irony here in the way the children are to be kept out.

Caesar i.e. Julius Caesar.
the topless towers The reference is to Ilium (Troy) in Marlowe's *Dr Faustus*.
a tinker shuffle i.e. like a tinker, a travelling salesman of tin- or copper-ware.
The first Adam i.e. sexual awakening.

A Bronze Head

A plaster cast of Maud Gonne. Four seven-line verses each ending in a rhyming couplet.

Hysterica passio See note p. 81 (the reference to *King Lear*).
McTaggart The philosopher who believed that things were 'composite' (1866–1925).
at the starting-post i.e. in her youth.
Propinquity Nearness in place, close kinship.
Ancestral pearls These three lines reflect Yeats's love of tradition and his attack on the destructive elements in his own society.

High Talk

A grotesque poem, in which the author writes in terms of 'stilts', which appear to approximate to his poetic form or the subjects he has used for poetry. He defends his usage on the ground that everyone is attracted to high things, and the whole poem in fact has a man-on-stilts-at-the-circus air about it. He then goes on to say that all that he has has 'run wild'.

Malachi A Hebrew prophet.

Why should not Old Men be Mad?

Again a poem about the past, written in short sardonic lines, the past colouring the 'old man' of the present. Some of the characters are readily identifiable, others not.

A girl … all Dante Iseult Gonne is meant here.
to bear children i.e. her husband (Francis Stuart).
A Helen of social welfare Appears to be a reference to Maud Gonne, but the next line makes one think it is more probably one of the women who took a militant part in the 1916 uprising or the civil war.

The Circus Animals' Desertion

Here Yeats reverts to the past, asking 'What can I but enumerate old themes?' His enumeration in this poem is superb – a meticulous control of the stanza form, and some telling self-analysis. The first verse looks at his early work, then in the second at his use of myth and legend to emphasize his own love. The next two deal with his plays, while the last speaks of where he has come to finally – 'the foul rag-and-bone shop of the heart'.

Circus animals ... stilted boys ... chariot i.e. the use of myth and legend in his early poems.
I thought my dear A reference to Maud Gonne, indelibly connected with *The Countess Cathleen* in Yeats's mind.
Fool ... Blind Man ... Cuchulain From *On Baile's Strand*, a play by Yeats.
A mound of refuse Despite the return to the 'heart', there is a great deal of bitterness here, perhaps expressive of the frustrations of old age and the feeling, from time to time present in Yeats, of his having achieved little.

Politics

Superb poem of old age, with the feeling of physical and romantic love still positive – a moment of wish-denial in time, caught and held in the words of the poem.

The Man and the Echo

Yeats here voices doubts about the effect his poetry had on those who read it. He asks himself whether he has transformed political passion into action and death, wonders whether he could have prevented the destruction of Coole Park. He is asking for answers to these questions.

Alt In Ben Bulben.
That play *Cathleen ni Houlihan* is meant here.
a house lay wrecked An obvious reference to Coole Park.
Lie down and die Note the ironic effect of the echo, which confirms his feelings as, indeed, it inevitably must.
bodkin A large needle with a large eye. Here seen as a weapon, probably a reference to *Hamlet* III, 1, 76.
Up there some hawk or owl The sounds of nature disturb the 'sounds' of an inward monologue, now become outward.

Under Ben Bulben

Finally Yeats returns to his central theme of decay and renewal – 'Gyres run on' – and there is a last rallying call to the Irish to manifest again their zest for life before we reach the celebrated epitaph. There is superb control of the short lines, a sweeping range of reference, with most of which we are familiar.

Mareotic Lake See note, p. 57.

the Witch of Atlas A poem by Shelley.

those horsemen Visions, visionary beings.

and ancient Ireland knew it all i.e. in the myths and legends he has written about.

Back in the human mind again i.e. through memory.

Mitchel's prayer A reference to John Mitchel's famous phrase, 'Give us war in our time, O Lord'.

Phidias See note, p. 64.

Michael Angelo See note, p. 85.

Can disturb globe-trotting Madam i.e. arouse her sexually, an ironic note here.

Calvert A Flemish painter.

Claude His first name, the second being Lorraine, French landscape painter.

Irish poets Note the range of Yeats's reference here in terms of what the Irish poets should take for their subjects.

Drumcliff A village in Sligo.

Revision Questions

1 Which of these poems do you find the most interesting and why?

2 Write a considered account of what you find are Yeats's main concerns in his later poems. You should quote in support of your views.

Revision questions

1 'Yeats chooses the most passionate experiences as subjects for his poems.' Consider this statement in the light of your reading of *Selected Poems*.

1. Guideline note-form answer:

(a) Introduction:
   The range of Yeats's subject-matter – his mystical and occult concerns (which were passionate to him) plus his youth of myth – tradition – contemporary events – personal love and feelings.

(b) Choose one poem under a particular heading – say three poems at least – and devote a paragraph to each one. In this paragraph you might consider *Easter 1916* as your focal point. You would need to bring out the nature of Yeats's passion with regard to individuals, events, the current climate of activity, repressive action, etc. Consider too the form of the poem.

(c) *Sailing to Byzantium* – passion for the past – for beauty – for the distance he has come – for art, learning, experience. The passion, both intellectual and emotional, as shown in the images and symbols used.

(d) *The Circus Animals' Desertion* – again a passion for the past, but here there is a note of cynicism, anger, frustration – the age theme (linked to impotence perhaps). Again look at the form of the poem.

(e) Conclusion – Yeats passionately involved in whatever he did and more particularly in his appraisal of the past, tradition, the contemporary events, the nature of art, the occult and mystical and, finally, the onset of age and its penalties.

2 Give, from your reading of the poems, any evidence you find of their having been composed aloud with the aim of their being read or sung aloud.

3 Show evidence of Yeats's love for Ireland, as evident in the poems in this *Selection*.

4 Write an essay on Yeats's use of symbols in his work.

5 Show, from your reading of Yeats's poetry, that he considered 'suffering' an essential part of the poetic experience.

6 Consider the themes of Youth and Age as you find them in his poetry.

7 Why do you think Yeats took so much care over the order of his poems in the various volumes?

8 Write an essay on his use of myth and legend.

9 How important do you think a knowledge of Yeats's life is to the understanding of his poetry.

10 'There is always vitality in the poetry of Yeats.' Do you agree?

11 'The dramatic writings of Yeats are echoed in his lyrics.' Do you find this to be the case?

12 Do you agree with Yeats's own belief that his poetry grew younger as he grew older?

13 Do you feel that politics can be considered a fit theme for poetry? Refer to specific poems in the *Selection*.

14 'A poet should sing rather than think.' Relate this statement to the *Selection*.

15 'Yeats is a poet of escape.' Consider this statement.

Further reading

W. B. Yeats: *Collected Plays*
W. B. Yeats: *Autobiographies*
Louis MacNeice: *The Poetry of W. B. Yeats*
A. Norman Jeffares: *Yeats: Man and Poet*
Richard Ellmann: *Yeats: The Man and the Masks*
T. R. Henn: *The Lonely Tower: Studies in the Poetry of W. B. Yeats*
A. G. Stock: *W. B. Yeats: His Poetry and Thought*
Jon Stallworthy: *Between the Lines: Yeats's Poetry in the Making*

Brodie's Notes

TITLES IN THE SERIES

Edward Albee	**Who's Afraid of Virginia Woolf?**
Jane Austen	**Emma**
Jane Austen	**Mansfield Park**
Jane Austen	**Pride and Prejudice**
Samuel Beckett	**Waiting for Godot**
William Blake	**Songs of Innocence and Experience**
Robert Bolt	**A Man for All Seasons**
Charlotte Brontë	**Jane Eyre**
Emily Brontë	**Wuthering Heights**
Geoffrey Chaucer	**The Franklin's Tale**
Geoffrey Chaucer	**The Knight's Tale**
Geoffrey Chaucer	**The Miller's Tale**
Geoffrey Chaucer	**The Nun's Priest's Tale**
Geoffrey Chaucer	**The Pardoner's Prologue and Tale**
Geoffrey Chaucer	**Prologue to the Canterbury Tales**
Geoffrey Chaucer	**The Wife of Bath's Tale**
Wilkie Collins	**Woman in White**
Joseph Conrad	**Heart of Darkness**
Charles Dickens	**Great Expectations**
Charles Dickens	**Hard Times**
Charles Dickens	**Oliver Twist**
Charles Dickens	**A Tale of Two Cities**
Gerald Durrell	**My Family and Other Animals**
George Eliot	**Silas Marner**
T. S. Eliot	**Selected Poems**
Henry Fielding	**Tom Jones**
F. Scott Fitzgerald	**The Great Gatsby** and **Tender is the Night**
E. M. Forster	**Howard's End**
E. M. Forster	**A Passage to India**
John Fowles	**The French Lieutenant's Woman**
Anne Frank	**The Diary of Anne Frank**
Mrs Gaskell	**North and South**
William Golding	**Lord of the Flies**
Graham Greene	**Brighton Rock**
Graham Greene	**The Power and the Glory**
Graham Handley (ed)	**The Metaphysical Poets: John Donne to Henry Vaughan**
Thomas Hardy	**Far From the Madding Crowd**
Thomas Hardy	**The Mayor of Casterbridge**
Thomas Hardy	**The Return of the Native**
Thomas Hardy	**Tess of the D'Urbervilles**
L. P. Hartley	**The Go-Between**
Aldous Huxley	**Brave New World**
James Joyce	**Portrait of the Artist as a Young Man**
John Keats	**Selected Poems and Letters of John Keats**
Philip Larkin	**Selected Poems of Philip Larkin**

D. H. Lawrence	The Rainbow
D. H. Lawrence	Sons and Lovers
D. H. Lawrence	Women in Love
Harper Lee	To Kill a Mockingbird
Laurie Lee	Cider with Rosie
Christopher Marlowe	Dr Faustus
Arthur Miller	The Crucible
Arthur Miller	Death of a Salesman
John Milton	Paradise Lost
Robert C. O'Brien	Z for Zachariah
Sean O'Casey	Juno and the Paycock
George Orwell	Animal Farm
George Orwell	1984
J. B. Priestley	An Inspector Calls
J. D. Salinger	The Catcher in the Rye
William Shakespeare	Antony and Cleopatra
William Shakespeare	As You Like It
William Shakespeare	Hamlet
William Shakespeare	Henry IV Part I
William Shakespeare	Julius Caesar
William Shakespeare	King Lear
William Shakespeare	Macbeth
William Shakespeare	Measure for Measure
William Shakespeare	The Merchant of Venice
William Shakespeare	A Midsummer Night's Dream
William Shakespeare	Much Ado about Nothing
William Shakespeare	Othello
William Shakespeare	Richard II
William Shakespeare	Romeo and Juliet
William Shakespeare	The Tempest
William Shakespeare	Twelfth Night
George Bernard Shaw	Pygmalion
Alan Sillitoe	Selected Fiction
John Steinbeck	Of Mice and Men and The Pearl
Jonathan Swift	Gulliver's Travels
Dylan Thomas	Under Milk Wood
Alice Walker	The Color Purple
W. B. Yeats	Selected Poetry

ENGLISH COURSEWORK BOOKS

Terri Apter	Women and Society
Kevin Dowling	Drama and Poetry
Philip Gooden	Conflict
Philip Gooden	Science Fiction
Margaret K. Gray	Modern Drama
Graham Handley	Modern Poetry
Graham Handley	Prose
Graham Handley	Childhood and Adolescence
R. J. Sims	The Short Story